SIMON de MONTFORT
Reformer and Rebel

SIMON de MONTFORT

Reformer and Rebel

by

Elizabeth Luckock

and

Caroline Gundry

Illustrated by

S. Thompson

WHEATON
A Member of the Pergamon Group

A WHEATON REFERENCE BOOK

Other books in this series:

THE CRUSADES
ROADS AND PIPE-LINES
BUYER BEWARE
TUNNELS AND BRIDGES
TELEVISION
THE MINOANS OF ANCIENT CRETE
THE FIRST WORLD WAR
THE EARLY DAYS OF MAN
SPANISH CONQUEST IN AMERICA
LIFE IN ANCIENT PERU
HISTORY ALL AROUND YOU
HOW TO BECOME A "PROFESSIONAL" AMATEUR DRESSMAKER
DAMS AND CANALS
WEIGHTS AND MEASURES – THEN AND NOW
SUMER AND BABYLON
ARCHÆOLOGY: SCIENCE AND ROMANCE
MYSTERIES OF ANIMAL BEHAVIOUR
WILLIAM THE CONQUEROR*
THE REIGN OF THE CONQUEROR*

* Also by Elizabeth Luckock

First published 1969
Library of Congress Catalog Card Number: 68–16587

Printed and bound in Great Britain by A. Wheaton & Co., Exeter

08 008757 4 Hard Cover
08 008236 6 Millboard

Simon de Montfort's seal

Contents

I

Rebels against the King

THROUGH the pale dawn of an early summer's day in May, 1264, a tall figure astride a great black warhorse led a small but resolute army up the winding tracks of the Sussex Downs outside the little town of Lewes. Simon de Montfort, stern, ascetic, black browed earl of Leicester, was about to launch himself into battle against his king, and there to fight, to the death if need be, for the cause to which he was pledged – the reform of the kingdom.

While encamped in the green forests of the Sussex Weald, he had received news that the king, with a great royalist force, was camped in Lewes town. Having sent those bishops who were with him and who believed in the rightness of his cause with a peace missive to the king, Earl Simon awaited a reply. When it came it breathed scorn, fury and defiance. King Henry III of England denounced Earl Simon and his followers as traitors and challenged them to do their worst.

And so the die was cast. After the years of crisis and the years of quarrels the ultimate defiance, the final severing of the feudal ties, had come at last. From now on Simon de Montfort and all who supported him could be called traitors and outlaws, and they would risk all the penalties incurred thereby – imprisonment, confiscation of property, death.

Marching silently through the dawn and gaining unseen the heights above the town while the king and all his chivalry slept below, this little army hurled itself down upon the hastily aroused royalist forces.

The bitter clang of arms rolled out over the Downs as the two armies clashed in mortal combat. The savage struggle thrashed to and fro as father struck at son and kinsman hacked at kinsman, for this was civil war. Finally the disciplined ardour of soul and will that inspired Earl Simon's smaller force showed its mastery and they emerged the victors of the battle. The king of England stood captive before the rebel earl, his near relation and once his dearest friend, and Simon de Montfort became the undisputed ruler of the land.

Triumphantly the proud victor rode to London, taking his royal captive with him. Everywhere on the road he was hailed with joy and enthusiasm, for even the poorest countryman felt that Simon was his friend and protector. The chance to put his cherished reforms into practice had arrived, for he was now the most powerful man in England. Before Christmas of that year, Earl Simon sent out writs summoning his supporters to a parliament in the New Year. Barons, churchmen, knights and burgesses were to attend. None but the humble villeins were forgotten.

On 20 January the parliament met, and how proudly Simon must have watched men from every corner of the realm converging on the capital. Cornishmen and Essex farmers, burghers from Bristol and countrymen from the Sussex Weald – all these gathered to discuss the peace between their leader and the king, and all hoped that their particular grievances would be resolved in the months that followed.

This was our most famous parliament because for the first time townspeople were summoned to attend it. It sat for two months and concerned itself only with agreeing on peace terms and on making less harsh the imprisonment of Prince Edward, a royal captive like his

father. Then, as the representatives set off, back to their towns and villages, Earl Simon journeyed to his home at Odiham for his last great family gathering. His enemies were surrounding him, many barons were leaving his side, and before long he would be fighting once more for his cause, this time to the death on the field of Evesham.

What had brought this earl of Leicester, by birth a foreigner and called by some an adventurer, to take up arms against his king and to become the most powerful man in England? What had brought him to become the hero of his adopted country, the champion of her liberties in one of the greatest of her constitutional struggles and the founder of the first of her democratically representative parliaments, which gave to English freedom its lasting shape? How did he become the man of whom Sir Winston Churchill wrote "He has lighted a fire never to be quenched in English history."?

For the beginnings of the story of the long struggle for power that culminated in this dramatic moment in England's history, we must go far back to 1066, when William of Normandy defeated another English king, Harold, at Hastings, and thereby forged a link between the neighbouring nations of France and England.

II

The King and his Barons

THE GREAT barons of medieval Europe were warriors above all else. Indeed they had to be, in an age when the sword held greater sway than the gentler arts of peace. These were the days when might decided right, and glory and honour could only be won on the battle-field. In these centuries a king's authority was based on his vigorous rule and his reputation as a warrior.

When Duke William of Normandy defeated Harold at Hastings in 1066, he linked England with the rest of Europe. There was no mass immigration of Normans; instead, it was a settlement of a baronial minority onto an existing structure. The lives of the town and country folk were hardly disrupted. The two powerful elements in the state were the monarch and the baronage. William's problem was that he had to give his barons sufficient power and resources to subjugate rebellious Anglo-Saxons and to bring England firmly under Norman rule. At the same time, he had to prevent their gaining too much independent power, which would threaten his position as monarch. He had to ensure that it was in the interests of his barons to support him as king. He succeeded in doing this through the introduction of feudalism, which bound the barons to him and he to the barons through their mutual contract. The basis of feudalism was the theory that all land belonged to the king. The

Knighting a young man.

chief barons held land from him: they were his tenants. But instead of paying him a money rent, they agreed to supply him with a certain number of knights, the number depending on the amount of land they held. Thus the king at one stroke provided himself with an army and by asserting his ownership of all land, he ensured that the barons and their vassals were dependent on him for their properties.

The feudal system touched every corner of English life. The barons were the active agents by whom all the operations of government were carried on. In the counties there were the baronial courts, where feudal law was administered and questions of land tenure decided. When William I began to establish a strong central government, the barons became his administrative officers and his justices. Above all, they formed the king's Great Council. It was their feudal duty owed to the king that they should act as his counsellors. Of course, it was impossible for this Great Council to meet very often; travel was difficult and expensive, and at any one time many magnates might be unable to attend. Three times a year the council met with great pomp and ceremony. At Christmas it met in Gloucester, at Easter in Winchester, and over Whitsun at Westminster. Here the bishops, abbots, foreign ambassadors and magnates were bidden, the latter with all their knights so that the king might discuss any new policies with them, and at the same time review the feudal host. "Discussion" here meant little more than to inform them of his decisions, for there was no idea of opposition or even of free debate. The king needed the co-operation of his baronage since they administered the country for him, and word of mouth was a better way of explaining a policy and ensuring co-operation than sending a written order round the countryside. In this way the making of the Domesday Survey was ordered at the Christmas Council of 1085.

Of course these councils had nothing to do with day-to-day government of the realm. Most decisions were made by men who were permanently with the king. Nor was the duty of counselling a popular one in the eleventh and twelfth centuries. There was little idea of public service. Many of the barons had lands in Normandy which had to be defended against the French. Others were concerned in wars on the Welsh and Scottish borders, or in travelling over their widely spread-out lands. As long as their own interests were protected they were satisfied.

In this way William I established the balance of power between the king and his barons. Although in practice the king was all-powerful, it was recognized that he ruled with the help of his magnates. The system did not always work very smoothly. Under a weak king such as Stephen, the barons fought and schemed against him and one another. But between 1100 and 1189, the accession of Henry I and death of Henry II respectively, much was done to strengthen the monarchy and to bring royal government right into the smallest communities, however far from the capital. The king's justices travelled the countryside, and anyone could take his case to a local royal court, or *curia regis*, if he paid a fee. Many did so, instead of using the old shire and baronial courts, because it was easier to obtain a just verdict in the king's courts. In this way, Henry II made possible the rapid

growth of a native system of law common to the whole land, in place of the mixture of Anglo-Saxon, Danish and Norman customs still administered in the shire and baronial courts. We call this new body of law the Common Law, because everyone, whatever his wealth or position, was subject to it. As the king's courts were the source of the Common Law, royal power was greatly increased, and this was often at the expense of the baronage.

These king's courts also dealt with the administration of the counties; in 1170, Henry II ordered a commission of travelling judges to direct an inquiry into the government of sheriffs and all local officials, whether servants of the king or of his barons. Many sheriffdoms had fallen into the hands of local magnates, and there was a danger that they might become hereditary in certain families. Frequent abuses of their power gave Henry the excuse to dismiss many of them and to appoint in their places obedient middle-class officials, who would be the executive agents of his will alone. This Inquest of Sheriffs, as it was called, was very important in centralizing royal power, for the sheriffs were the link between central and local government.

Henry II reduced the power of the barons in other ways too. He asserted his right to garrison private castles with his own men. He reorganized the militia of the shires by the Assize of Arms, and put it under the command of his sheriffs and justices instead of the earls. He created new barons, men sufficiently important to act as a check upon the older families but not strong enough to be a menace to the crown. By the end of his reign he had gone far towards replacing the feudal system of administration and justice with a new, more modern idea. He was using professional men to help him govern, and the barons, his traditional counsellors, were losing their status as governors of the realm.

III

Magna Carta

HENRY II had built up the power of the crown very much at the expense of the baronage. Yet his work was generally popular, and even in the great feudal rebellion of 1174 the barons were not united against him. After all, Henry's legal reforms guaranteed them their tenancy of land against him, just as they guaranteed the lesser tenants their land against the barons. Few men wanted a return to the anarchy of Stephen's reign for there was no advantage in disorder. In such an event rents were lost and there was a general decline in prosperity and security, as neighbours and families fought one another, no property being considered sacred.

Henry had called together his feudal Great Council frequently, for he saw no difficulty in obtaining the baron's consent to his schemes. Yet in spite of frequent meetings together the barons showed few signs that they were becoming conscious of their place in politics. They did not try to give this feudal court a definite place in the government of the country by making it a regular and permanent institution, nor did they claim that they had the greatest right to counsel their king. In 1189, all that seems to have been important to them was the feudal contract with its mutual obligations to king and vassals. They were too occupied fighting in Normandy, Poitou or Aquitaine, or in crusading, to spare much thought for theories of government. How then, did this seemingly calm situation change so drastically between Henry II's death in 1189 and 1215, when John was forced by a united baronage to put his seal to Magna Carta?

The growth of royal power under Henry II had been necessary for the preservation of peace and order in England. Henry had used his power wisely and had always observed the feudal contract. The balance between monarch and baronage, those two most powerful elements in the community, had been preserved, though the king was now indisputably the master. Richard I, who succeeded his father in 1189, and later John his brother, upset that balance by abusing their power, and eventually drove the magnates into united opposition, which resulted in Magna Carta, a treaty between John and his vassals.

Left: *The effigy on the tomb of Henry II at Fontevrault, France.*

Below: *The effigy on the tomb of Richard I at Fontevrault, France.*

Richard I, Cœur de Lion, loved war and idolized the chivalric order. Despising the arts of peace and totally unlike his unostentatious and diplomatic father, he personified ideal kingship to his warrior barons. Between 1189 and his death in 1199, he spent five months in England. He was an ardent crusader, and during those ten years the English had to supply great sums of money to finance the Holy War, and eventually to pay a huge ransom for him when he was captured by the Austrian emperor on his way home in 1194. Although enormous taxation did not precipitate active baronial opposition, the foundations of unrest had been laid. In 1197, Richard called upon the barons to furnish 300 knights for a year's service in France instead of the usual feudal levy, but this was refused by the Great Council as being illegal, and the plan failed. Obviously there was a growing disposition to watch the king's conduct and to make sure he kept within the law as defined by the feudal contract.

It was King John who really provoked the final crisis. To begin with, he was a very unattractive character, the complete opposite to the chivalric ideal. Unsuccessful in war, he was soon nicknamed "Soft Sword" by the barons. The chroniclers of the time describe him as being vicious and sadistic, a man who would betray his friends if there was any gain thereby for himself. His incredible duplicity and underhand dealings soon lost him most baronial support, and it is said that when he signed Magna Carta in 1215, only seven knights were still true to him.

John's reign very forcibly demonstrated to the barons that there must be some defined limit to royal power. It seemed to them that the monarchy was dangerously close to becoming irresponsibly despotic. John, obsessed with the idea of regaining his Angevin empire, sought every means of extorting money out of his barons and people, to finance his wars abroad. In 1212 he held a great inquiry into tenures and the consequent liabilities of his

The effigy on the tomb of King John at Worcester cathedral.

vassals, so that he might squeeze every penny out of their obligations to him. Later he went beyond the law, demanding illegal aids and frequent scutages, and abusing his rights of wardship and marriage. Estates were confiscated on the flimsiest of pretexts unless their owners paid large sums to the king, and John even demanded hostages from some of the more powerful barons, presumably hoping thereby to ensure their loyal support. It is hardly surprising that a baronial opposition party soon developed and the question arose of how this tyranny should be ended and a means found of returning to lawful government.

On 17 June 1215 a great concourse of barons and prelates gathered on one bank of the Thames at Runnymede. Led by Stephen Langton, archbishop of Canterbury, they must have seemed a formidable gathering,

their armour glinting in the sunlight, as they faced King John and his small body of supporters encamped on the opposite bank. Then, on an island in mid-river, the king met his opponents, and put his seal to a document that began the establishment of a limited monarchy in England. This was Magna Carta, so called not because contemporaries foresaw its enormous importance in the years to come, but because of its great length, and to distinguish it from the Charter of the Forests, issued in the following year.

The barons were not suggesting new methods of government; they were insisting on a return to the full observance of the feudal contract. Magna Carta is primarily a feudal document, devoted to the definition of feudal duties and privileges. The former vagueness of these had made it easy for kings to exploit them fully. Yet in defining the feudal contract the barons were re-emphasizing the principle that even monarchs must rule under the law. They were not irresponsible rulers, but custodians of ancient law and custom. As in Henry I's Coronation Charter, there was a demand for a return to a seemingly ideal past when the laws of Edward the Confessor reigned supreme. The barons recognized the need for strong central government, but they insisted that the king must submit himself to the same rules that he imposed on others. They demanded from him the same regularity of procedure and treatment that he was demanding from them. No longer could he break, ignore or suspend laws at his own convenience, for he must rule according to the law, and not above it. In this principle lies the whole basis of limited constitutional monarchy.

The "freemen" of the Charter whose liberties were there guaranteed belong to a feudal concept. The term takes in all except villeins, all in fact who held their land by free tenure. The mass of lesser knights and gentry could not be ignored since much of the administrative machinery of the country lay in their hands. But the barons saw themselves as the natural representatives of the community of the realm. They were not really interested in the rights of lesser men, only in their own liberties and privileges as secured between themselves and the king. Their interests in 1215 were entirely selfish. What is going to be important when we look at their struggles in the thirteenth century is the fact that in 1215 they were acting as a national class, pursuing a a common aim, and not as groups of individuals following entirely personal interests.

In Magna Carta the barons were not trying to limit the king through insisting that he could not act without their approval. The committee of twenty-four which they set up was not for the purpose of government, but to act as a court to which appeal might be made against breaches of the charter. As yet, they did not claim a part to play in the government of the realm, other than their rather vague rôle as feudal counsellors. In Henry III's reign it became obvious that the feudal limitations on royal power were not enough to ensure good government in the interests of the whole community, and the baronage had to go a step further and attempt to change the constitution. Magna Carta might be called the last fling of political feudalism.

IV

The Charter Re-issued

In October 1216 King John died at Newark after an orgy of peaches and new cider. He left his realm in a state of civil war, with all the east and south-east controlled by the invader, Louis of France, who had crossed the Channel at the invitation of the rebel barons. It was a bad time for a new king, and Henry III was only a boy of nine, but even so the barons must have greeted news of John's death with relief, and perhaps too there was an optimistic feeling that with a fresh reign a new era of justice and good government would begin.

On 28 October the child Henry was crowned king in Gloucester abbey. "Standing before the high altar," wrote the St Albans chronicler, "with Jocelin, bishop of Bath, dictating the oath, he swore in the presence of clergy and people . . . that he would give honour, peace and reverence to God and His Holy Church and its ministers all the days of his life. He swore that he would show strict justice to the people committed to him, that he would destroy evil laws and unjust customs, and would observe the good and make everyone else observe them." Then the young king was crowned with a golden bracelet of his mother's, all the royal treasure and crown having been lost with King John's baggage whilst he was crossing the Wash.

King John had entrusted his son to the care of the pope, represented in England by Gualo the Legate, and to William the Marshall, who for twenty years had been a tower of strength to the crown. Even in the troubles of King John's reign, William's loyalty had never wavered. He had taken the part of a peacemaker in the discussions before the sealing of Magna Carta, and his reputation for wisdom and moderation went far towards reconciling rebels and royalists. One of his first acts was to re-issue the Charter, and to promise a full pardon and restitution of land to all who would submit to the king. By the end of 1217 Louis had left England and the French fleet had been destroyed off Sandwich. This victory was celebrated by another confirmation of Magna Carta, and by the issue of the Charter of the Forests, which greatly curtailed the area of the royal forests, lessened the power of the forest courts and imposed checks on the activities of their officials.

These re-issues of Magna Carta, which appeared in 1216 and 1217, are not identical to the original document of 1215. The first of them was issued at a time when the marshal was anxious to re-affirm the power of the crown, and any clause that seemed to impose undue restrictions on royal rights was omitted. For this

Magna Carta.

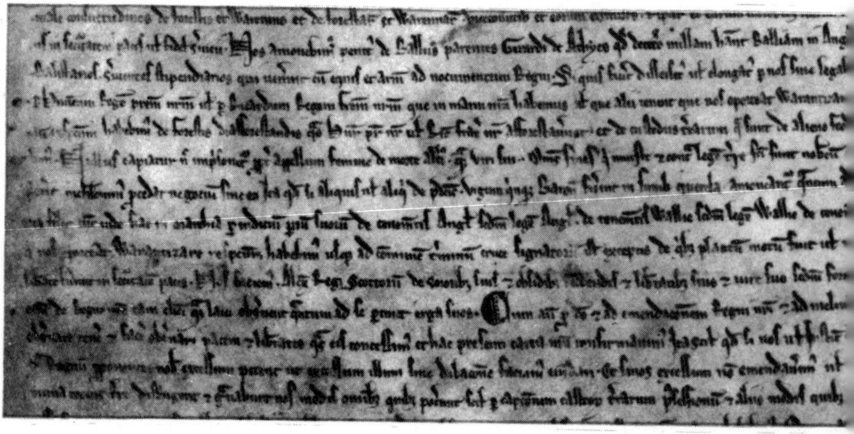

reason, the clause that recognized the right of the Great Council to control taxation disappeared, probably because the marshal did not want to restrict his powers of raising money for the war against Louis and the rebels. The 1217 re-issue added new clauses which reflected the power of the baronage in the then re-united kingdom. The Charter was re-modelled, its feudal character being even more clearly apparent than in 1215.

Yet these changes are not really important compared with more far-reaching results of the civil war. On the one hand, it was to make future kings dread national resistance to their actions, so that they would always consult their Great Council before imposing new or heavy taxation; on the other hand, it was to make them thoroughly distrustful of their baronage so that under Henry III the magnates were to be excluded from the administration, and shut out from all effective power. Lack of good will between Henry and his barons prevented the co-operation between them which was needed for good and stable government.

In 1219 William the Marshall died, leaving behind him not only a reputation for unflinching loyalty to his monarch, but also a realm that was at least outwardly

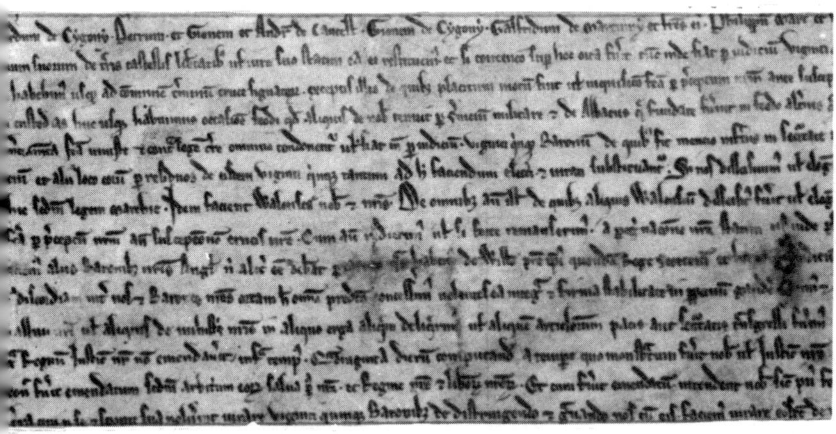

united under the crown. But the calm was only skin-deep. After his death, many of the bolder barons began to throw off the restraints of law and to terrorize their neighbours and the countryside around. The story of Falkes de Breaute shows how lawless and violent some of these barons could be. He had been bad King John's right-hand man, and as such had been rewarded with everything his master had to offer. He was sheriff of six counties and had the custody of several castles, notably that of Bedford. This he entrusted to his rascally brother William, who actually ventured to imprison one of the king's judges because he had condemned him to pay a fine at the assizes. This was too much, and the justiciar, Hubert de Burgh, marched to besiege Bedford castle. Eventually William de Breaute and his garrison surrendered and were hanged, whilst Falkes was exiled from England, never to return.

These were the sort of people with whom those in search of orderly government had to contend. Hubert de Burgh, who had held chief power since the death of William the Marshall, was stern and resolute in putting down what he considered evil. He continued William's work by getting all the important castles back into the king's hands, and by ridding England of the many foreign mercenaries who had fought for King John against the barons. He prohibited tournaments, sent out commissioners to do summary justice upon highway robbers, and did not shrink from repressing the most powerful of feudal magnates. His rule was just, and he had the welfare of England at heart, but in 1232 he was driven from power by the bishop of Winchester, and the administration entrusted to the hands of foreigners, chief among these being the bishop's nephew, Peter des Rievaulx.

V

Government without the Barons

HENRY III reached his full majority at the beginning of 1227. In 1221 he had been crowned again, this time with all pomp and ceremony at Westminster. During the six years following this, the king was finding his feet and asserting himself. His was not a very decisive character. Though intelligent and princely in his bearing, he was too hot-tempered, impulsive and easily distracted to make a great monarch. He had no military tendencies, and no special political ideas, and he did not command respect either from his government or from his barons. He was easily frightened and would swing quickly from one opinion to another depending on which adviser saw him last. His courtiers nicknamed him "Wax Heart". It was difficult to trust him, and his affectionate, clinging nature made it possible for him to be greatly influenced by those whom he admired. Needless to say, he was a poor judge of character.

Henry's character did not endear him to the baronage. They were a turbulent warrior class; he loved beauty and craftmanship, paying attention to detail in dress, decoration and ceremonial. There was more of the Latin than the Anglo-Saxon in him, and perhaps this was why he liked the company of foreigners. A fondness for extravagant display was one of his faults, but it was more than redeemed by his creative and artistic abilities. He

The likeness of Henry III on his tomb in Westminster abbey.

loved to design beautiful buildings and, having a keen interest in sanitation, combined practical as well as aesthetic details, such as the channel at Westminster palace designed to carry away all dirty water from the king's kitchen. Westminster abbey still stands as his greatest monument; the England that he left was more beautiful than that to which he had come.

How was this England governed in 1227? First, there

was the king. All government officials were his servants, and none had independence of action outside his wishes. Then there were the great officers of state: the justiciar, who acted for the king in his absence, and could issue writs in his own rather than the king's name; the chancellor, who supervised the chancery and its staff of clerks; and the treasurer, in charge of finance and the exchequer. But since the king had to travel around the countryside a great deal, and had to carry his administration with him, and since these great government departments were far too cumbersome to move around, there evolved a smaller body of royal officials, who dealt with day-to-day administration and who were centred on the king's household. Thus household government co-ordinated with the great departments, both being dominated by the king.

As government became more complicated and the scope of business increased, so professional men were needed as civil servants. The baronage, unpractised in the art of government, became increasingly estranged from the central administration, but they still had their duty of counsel in the *curia regis*, and a link with the government through the great offices of state, for these were usually filled by barons or great churchmen.

Hubert de Burgh was the last great justiciar. Future kings were going to spend more time in England now that their continental possessions were fewer, and there would be little need for the vice-regal office. There was another reason too. Henry III was not a strong king and he feared his barons. He was also under the influence of the French-born bishop of Winchester, Peter des Roches. It was largely through this man's work that Hubert lost power in 1232. From then on the king's personal household ruled England, the great offices of state became empty honours with little power, and their duties were performed by subordinates actually in the household. The latter not only supervised the administration of government, but shaped new policies as well. Suddenly the baronage seemed to be completely out of touch with the government, with no way either of influencing it or of curtailing its activities.

In 1232 Peter des Rievaulx, a foreigner and nephew of the bishop of Winchester, was made keeper of the king's wardrobe and chamber and treasurer of the household. Thus all branches of the household were governed by one man, and under him its influence grew. In 1238, the chancery lost all effective power when its Great Seal was taken from it and entrusted to wardrobe clerks. Without the seal, the chancellor's writs had no validity. The Great Seal was the key to power, and Henry now had direct control of it, and even took it abroad with him in 1242.

At the same time taxes and other payments which before would have gone to the exchequer were now transferred to the smaller wardrobe treasury, also in the king's control. As the thirteenth century progressed, so the wardrobe grew and mastered more of the government. It was an efficient administration and during Henry's reign there was rapid development of the methods of government, which grew increasingly complicated as England became a closer-knit and more prosperous nation. But Henry made several mistakes, and these earned him the opposition of the magnates.

The barons were left outside this development of Henry's government. He not only did not consult his barons, but he gave all power to foreigners – "adventurers" as they were termed by the jealous magnates. These Frenchmen, often the king's or queen's relatives, were deeply resented by a baronage that was growing increasingly conscious of its English nationality. The foreigners seemed to pour across the Channel, and were rewarded with estates, powerful positions and often the hand of an English heiress.

Naturally the barons resented the intrusion of foreigners and felt that their positions as counsellors to the king were being usurped. There were other grievances too. King Henry loved fine clothes and ceremonial, and when

it came to royal great occasions his extravagance was unsurpassed. Indeed life at court was very frivolous in these years. Frolics, dancing and pageants were the order of the day. Minstrels and jugglers were in high favour. How irritating it must have been to the rough and ready English barons not only to be dismissed as uncouth by the king's foreign favourites, but also to see such extravagant spending of the country's wealth, and with no advantage to themselves!

Henry's policies were also the subject of great criticism. He had a weakness for embarking on expensive foreign enterprises, which, even if they had succeeded in their aims, were not in England's interests. Though himself a peaceable man, he was easy prey for foreign advisers who had their own interests and ambitions at heart. The barons bitterly criticized his policies. Between 1232 and 1258 they were continually being asked to supply money for schemes on which their advice was never sought. Gradually they began to form a united opposition, with clearer ideas on the sorts of reforms needed; there was a new consciousness of the duties of the king, and the part they themselves should play in the government of the country. They were forced to consider how they should control the king, and force him to rule in the nation's interests.

All over Europe during the thirteenth century the idea was growing up that kingship was an office, its chief function being to serve the interests of the community. No longer did the people regard their king chiefly as a lord of vassals, with the kingdom as his estate, to be exploited as he wished. The interests of the nation could be quite contrary to the king's personal interests, and it was for the nation that he existed. In the old days, it had been accepted that the king's natural counsellors were his barons, and that they should advise him and help to further his ends. But Henry III was ruling without his barons, and the nation was suffering from his bad advisers and foolhardy policies. Although he summoned his feudal council fairly often, he did not ask their advice or take them into his confidence, and sometimes did not even attend their assemblies, sending a clerk to address them in his place.

Slowly the barons began to realize that they could no longer expect the old feudal methods of government to work. Instead of trying to resurrect the feudal conception of government by king and *curia regis*, they must fashion a new constitution that would give them fresh control over the activities of the government. In order to make themselves felt, they must approach the administration from without, and must negotiate with it. Before 1250 the term "parliament" begins to appear, meaning to talk or "parley". But to negotiate one must be at least as powerful as one's adversary, and so from 1240 on we see the baronage trying to strengthen itself by forming a compact body of opposition to the crown, and asserting that it represented the whole body of the king's tenants-in-chief.

All this was to happen very slowly, and the Provisions of Oxford, accepted by Henry in 1258, were only a great step in the barons' efforts to give themselves a decisive part in the formation and execution of royal policies.

VI

The Provisions of Oxford

In 1258 matters came to a speedy crisis. King Henry had involved England in yet another hare-brained scheme for which much money was needed. He had accepted the papal offer of the Sicilian crown for his younger son Edmund, and the conditions attached to the gift made this a very foolish step. For years the pope had nourished the ambition of adding Sicily to the papal dominions, and since Henry was a loyal vassal it was a good idea to make his son its monarch. But Henry had promised not only to provide an army against the other claimant, but also to provide a huge sum of money to finance the war. In his wildest imagination he could not have seen any profit for England in such an expensive undertaking. He was obliged to turn to his barons for funds, and called a parliament which met at Westminster in April 1258. Of course the barons were furious that the king should have involved the realm in such a reckless adventure without first consulting them, and in a secret meeting they promised to stand together in all things, and to resist with determination the royal demands for money. Confronted by his barons in warlike mood and dress, the king fearfully agreed to hold another parliament at Oxford in June, which would arrange to reform the state of the country before the end of the year.

In return the barons declared that they would do their best to persuade the community to grant aid for the Sicilian enterprise.

Two months later the Mad Parliament, as it was called, met in Oxford. Again the whole body of barons was collected together and fully armed, and with this display of might the king could hardly do other than accept their scheme for reform. These plans were called the Provisions of Oxford.

The reforms outlined in the Provisions of Oxford were drawn up by a committee of twenty-four men, half of these being chosen by King Henry, and half by the barons. Firstly there was to be a council of fifteen members, who were to advise Henry on all matters relating to the government of the country and to make itself responsible for the redress of all abuses of government. This council was to be elected by four people, two representatives of the barons and two of the king's party. It was to be a permanent advisory council, and to hold all authority. The king was bound to act as this council wished.

The great offices of state were to be restored to their old rank and power, and again made independent of the king and his household. The justiciar, chancellor and treasurer were responsible to the council of fifteen, and they were to hold office for one year only. The treasurer was to see that national revenues were paid into the exchequer and not diverted into the king's private treasury, as had been happening previously. In local government, too, officials were to be placed under control, and a careful investigation made into all complaints of official misconduct. All the principal ministers and judges were to be chosen with the approval of the barons, and all foreigners holding lands, castles and revenues granted them by the king were to give them up to Englishmen. The king's foreign "advisers" were to be replaced as well, and they were to be expelled from the kingdom.

What happened to the old feudal council or *curia regis?* Most certainly it was not forgotten in 1258. As we have seen, since about 1190 the old co-operation between the king and his vassals was slowly disappearing. Bad and irresponsible rule under John and Henry III had destroyed it, for the barons now saw that it was no longer in their interests to be willing servants and supporters of the crown. Instead they had begun to distrust and criticize their monarch and to form a will of their own. In 1258 the feudal council was given a place in the government, in which it was to be the link between governors and governed. Representing the whole body of tenants-in-chief, it was to watch the administration from a distance, informing it about the state of the community. There were to be three parliaments every year, and at these twelve barons, representing their fellows, were to meet and talk with the permanent council. Whatever was decided at these Great Councils was thereafter to bind the community.

The Provisions of Oxford were unsuccessful in their attempt to create a new and efficient government in which the king's power of independent action was strictly controlled by the baronage. Under the new system all authority was given to the permanent council of fifteen. But there was no place in it for a single leader who was sufficiently detached to unify all other interests behind him. The barons' party consisted of many individuals with different interests, and the only thing that united them all in 1258 was hatred and jealousy of Henry's foreign favourites, and disgust at his inefficient and wasteful government.

They had acted so as to put an end to this situation, and to give themselves the place that they felt they should rightly have in the administration. In doing this they had promised to remedy abuses in central and local government, and at first they did introduce measures of reform, ordering knights of the shires to draw up lists of unjust practices and grievances to submit to the government. But then they discovered that remedy of these abuses was against their own interests, since they themselves had been profiting from them on their own estates. They had acted to give themselves more power and influence, and many of them were not prepared to lose any privileges, nor were they really interested in bettering the lot of their lesser tenants. Only a few men, such as Simon de Montfort, looked further than the immediate and selfish aims of their fellow barons and genuinely wished for all freemen to benefit from their reforms. Thus the baronial party quickly broke up into rival factions, and they quarrelled much among themselves. In 1260 the earl of Gloucester and his party went over to the royal side, after bitter quarrels with Simon de Montfort, and this gave Prince Edward the chance of building up a royalist party liberal enough to attract many of the more moderate barons who were royalist at heart. In 1261 the king was absolved by the pope from his promise to observe the Provisions of Oxford, and the new government disappeared. But neither the reformers nor the royalists were going to surrender, and in May 1264, as we shall see, they met on the field of Lewes, and civil war had begun.

VII

The Church and the Friars

HAVING given a sketch of the history that led up to the struggle between Henry III and Simon de Montfort, let us now try to sketch the scene in which the struggle was to be set and see how the different classes of people who took part in the struggle had grown up.

Back in the days of Henry II the royal dominions stretched from Northumbria to the Pyrenees. Half of what is today France was King Henry's inheritance. England was only a large province in this empire, and it was chiefly a source of supply for soldiers and funds with which to defend his continental frontiers against the king of France. Henry himself was not an Englishman, and spent only a small proportion of his reign in England. With such spread-out dominions he had to travel a great deal, and his ever moving court was filled with men of business, pleasure and scholarship from all over western Europe.

Few "Englishmen" in Henry's reign were conscious of their nationality or that England was a nation itself. France, Germany, Italy, England – all these were part of the same culture, and the great men of each land communicated easily with each other in French, the language of the court, or Latin, the language of the church. What in fact was an Englishman in 1150? Was he the

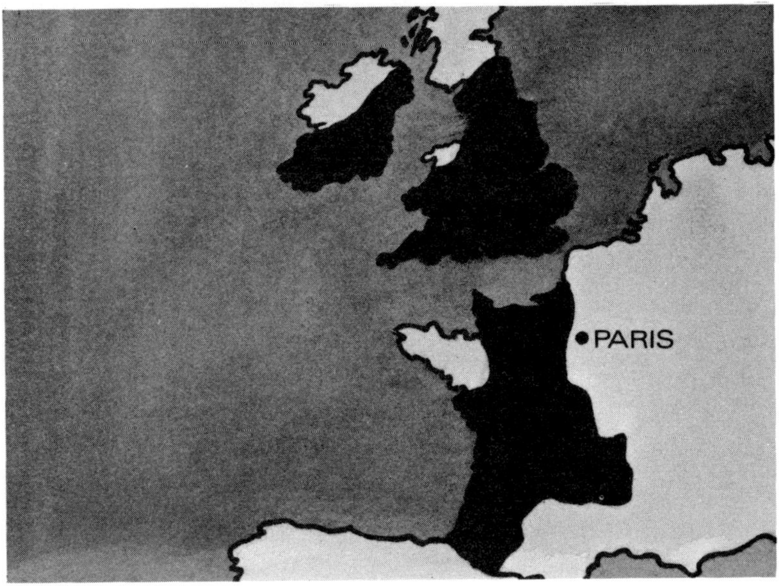

The dominions of Henry II.

Celt of wild Wales, or the Anglo-Saxon who had conquered him, or the Norman baron who held lands in France as well? These racial differences died out slowly as Anglo-Saxon women married Norman soldiers, but it took a long time for a feeling of common nationality to develop, in which people would see themselves as all belonging to one great and independent nation, England.

In 1204 King John was defeated by the French king, Philip Augustus, and lost Normandy. Barons who had held lands in Normandy and England now had to choose between their allegiance to the French and English crowns. They could not pay homage to both kings, and many forfeited their Norman estates. From now onwards their possessions and homes were on English soil alone and so they began to interest themselves in English questions and issues, and to take on a more purely English outlook. They felt more pride in their island realm, and were concerned that it should be ruled in the best interests of the community. At first their "community" was a narrow section of all Englishmen, for it included only their own class, but as trade grew and more people entered public life through local government so other classes began to gain in importance, and to become more conscious of the nation to which they all belonged. Itinerant justices who toured the land provided a strong link between Westminster and even the most far-flung shires. People began to travel more, so that fewer communities were isolated and unaware of events affecting the whole country.

The roads, often legacies from Roman times, were full of travellers; pilgrims journeying to distant shrines, such as that of St Thomas à Becket at Canterbury; barons moving between their estates; countrymen going to their local shire courts, and cartloads of heavy goods being taken to and from the ports. These roads were not good: in 1294 it took nine days for twenty-one cartloads of treasure to travel from London to Norwich. Carters often had to hire extra help because "of the depth of the ways and the weakness of the horses".

As people began to consider themselves as all belonging to one nation, so they began to feel proud of their nationality, and to resent foreigners who were given estates and power by the king. They also resented the Italian priests sent from Rome to govern the church. England's wealth, they felt, should be for the English; neither the king's foreign relations nor the pope had any right to the rewards of English prosperity.

At this time the pope, attempting to raise a regular income from England, was making outrageous claims and demanding vast sums from the English clergy and people. Already he received 1,000 marks a year as overlord and £199 8s in Peter's Pence, paid in a certain fixed sum for each diocese, but these sums were not enough to support his enormous expenditure. All sorts of dues were levied and these were increased again and again. Whenever a well-paid office fell vacant in the church some dispute arose about who was to occupy it.

For example, on the death of Archbishop Stephen Langton in 1228, the monks of St Augustine's priory at Canterbury asked if one of their number might be appointed to the office. But the pope set aside this candidate for a nominee of his own. In less than fifty years no fewer than thirty contested elections for English bishoprics were carried to Rome for decision and in every case heavy fees had to be paid.

The sale of livings in the church was carried on in a bare-faced manner. The highest bidder for a clerical office almost invariably got it, without any regard to his fitness for it. Whole hordes of foreign ecclesiastics were sent over from the Continent to fill English vacancies, and in many cases they did not even live in the country. They remained abroad and had the revenues of their livings sent out to them, whilst a poor, ill-paid priest carried out the duties. On one occasion 300 Italian priests arrived and the legate was told that no benefices were to be filled by Englishmen until all these foreigners had been provided for.

As the pope's demands grew larger and more frequent, so anti-papal feeling grew in England. Such saintly and learned churchmen as Edmund of Abingdon and Grosseteste of Lincoln spoke out openly against irreligious men being given responsible positions in the church. The English clergy resented the taxes they were forced to send to Rome. Amid the rumblings of political discontent in England, a new body of dissent was making itself heard. It was very unfortunate that King Henry did not support these clerics against the pope, as his forbear Henry II had done. However, he was himself a very pious man; it is said that every day he would hear three masses. His very great religious feeling made it difficult for him to oppose the pope. Besides, it was from the pope that he received his throne after his father's death. Loyalty to the church, and to its head, was second nature to him. Had he resisted some of the pope's more exorbitant demands he might have won over many of the clergy to the royalist side, but he did not, and so they were ready and willing to support Simon de Montfort in 1258.

It was during these sordid squabbles between the pope and the English clergy that a change little short of a religious revolution was being introduced into England by the arrival of the mendicant friars of the orders of St Francis and St Dominic. The awakening of the English people to political life so that they eventually demanded and obtained a share in the government of their country was largely due to the preaching and influence of these friars who came to England in the thirteenth century.

The various orders of monks already in England had done much good work with their magnificent building, their reclaiming of and cultivating of waste land, and their improvement of livestock. They had dispensed charity and had preserved learning and literature in a rough and warlike age. Their ideal had been retirement and separation from the everyday world of men. They cut themselves off from ordinary affairs such as business and war, and gave themselves up to prayer and meditation and study. The parish priests looked after the spiritual welfare of the ordinary people while the monks looked after their own souls. This worked as long as the country was chiefly rural, but as men began to crowd more and more to the towns the system broke down, and so the arrival of the Franciscans and Dominicans in 1221 and 1224 respectively helped to fill an important gap in the work of the church.

The two founders of these orders, St Dominic and St Francis, had been struck with two phases of life with which the church, as it then existed, seemed powerless to deal. St Dominic, the Spaniard, orthodox, rigid, dogmatic, mourned the heresy that he saw spreading among the bourgeois population of the towns. He believed that the only remedy for it was to be found in an order of popular preachers – men who should be able to meet the heretical ministers on their own ground – and who should show by their devotion, their poverty and their learning that christianity had something more to offer than was apparent in the lives of gorgeous prelates wholly absorbed in church business, or fat monks and abbots whose highest ideal was to withdraw themselves into the solitude and sanctity of their cloisters and to leave the rest of the world to get on as best it could.

The Italian St Francis, on the other hand, was struck, not with the heresy of the upper classes, but with the irreligion and misery of the squalid masses whom the growth of commerce and the tyranny of the rural nobility were forcing to crowd into the towns.

Monks were supposed never to leave their cloisters, but the friars of St Francis had no cloisters to leave. Even when they had nowhere to lay their heads their life work was not to save their own souls, but first and foremost to save the souls and bodies of others. They were to go among the people, ministering to the sick, teaching the ignorant and preaching to the careless and the irreligious in the language of the day, which they could understand.

Soon every town in England had its friary built in the lowest slums and from it there issued forth a band of men eager to help their neighbours in every possible way. In

their long robes of coarse grey cloth with girdles of rope around their waists, they begged their bread from house to house, ministering to the poor, the outcasts and the lepers.

St Francis had in the beginning discouraged his followers from studying, and wished them to devote themselves entirely to a life of action. Before long, however, they found that if they were really to help the diseased, the lepers and the maimed, they must study anatomy and the science of medicine, and in doing so they became the first physicists; they also found that if they were to cope with the sharp wits of the townspeople, they must not neglect their logic and learning. Consequently they began to flock to the universities, and it was through the activities of the Franciscans that Oxford became famous throughout Europe.

The influence of such a body as the Franciscans was enormous, for the friars held in the thirteenth century the position now held by the press. Their sermons took the place of the leading article, and the arrival of a friar from Oxford or London was the event of the day: his opinions represented the latest news and, as he was thoroughly democratic in habits and tone, his influence gave an enormous impetus to the spread of popular ideas and the formation of public opinion.

The friars urged the responsibility of the king towards God and his duty to rule for the good of his subjects, and these views they proclaimed in the market-place. King Henry III, showing his displeasure, declared that the friars were going too far and turning men's heads. But in the opinion of historians it was the Franciscans who were largely responsible for a general political awakening, and for making a far greater part of the population consider how they should be governed, and with what aims. It was this that gained for the barons the support of the people against the king in the struggles of the mid-thirteenth century. Public opinion was beginning to be educated.

VIII

The Knights of the Shires

IF WE were to be given a bird's-eye view of the whole of England in 1200, we should see a very different picture from that existing today. In place of our large cities with their sprawling suburbs and forests of factory chimneys and office buildings, we should see smaller, more closely grouped clusters of buildings, often with a wall neatly surrounding them as protection from marauders or the foreign invader. In place of our patchwork of intensively cultivated farming land stretching over all the countryside except the poorest regions of hill and bog-land, we should see countless village communities, each surrounded by its farming land, but often separated from neighbouring villages by stretches of uncultivated wasteland or of royal forest. In place of our network of tarmac roads we should see a few great highways, built by the Romans, but mostly only dirt roads, connecting with each other by way of smaller roads or tracks, along which a cart or horseman might take many days to travel.

England in 1200 was a land of isolated and independent communities. News took a long time to travel from London or Bristol to the villages of Norfolk or Devon, and a piece of news generally reached its destination via several mouths, and gained all sorts of inaccuracies on the way. There was no printed word till the end

of the fifteenth century – indeed had there been any, few people would have been able to read it, and those Englishmen who could have might have found it written in French, the language of the court, or Latin, the language of church and administration.

In the thirteenth century each village formed an almost independent unit. Produce from their land gave the villagers sufficient food for their simple diet, and any surplus they took to their nearest market or fair, to barter for those necessities of life which they could not themselves supply. Most villagers rarely travelled, except to the markets in their local towns. Their view of life was essentially a simple one, which did not stretch far from their native countryside, each year producing its regular pattern of seasonal change, the church strongly in the background with its promise of eternal life for the devout, and its warnings of hell-fire for the wicked.

Yet gradually all these tiny communities were establishing stronger links with Westminster and their king.

Before 1066 the Anglo-Saxon system of local government depended on the ability of local people to look after their own affairs. Each community was in practice independent, since the whole country was seldom strongly united under one king and there was thus no central government with the influence and means to supervise the affairs of the whole kingdom. Many people felt stronger loyalties towards their local region than towards the rather unreal idea of a kingdom of England.

After 1066 the same system of administration in shire and hundred continued, but in many cases the offices in local government changed hands. William I depended on his warrior barons for co-operation in running his new kingdom, and so these barons were often given the positions and responsibilities hitherto held by Anglo-Saxons of local importance. The barons' courts did not entirely replace the old shire courts but they took over many of the duties of the latter.

It was in the interest of these barons to render loyal

service to the king. If they were treacherous and selfish, as many were in the century that followed, they stood in danger of losing their lands and positions. In this way William restored a strong central power to a country that had been greatly divided by diverse loyalties and varying local interests since the days of King Canute.

In the century and a half that followed the Norman conquest, successive kings sought to build up royal power at the expense of their chief vassals. Once the Norman monarchy was strongly established and the English subjugated, they deliberately began to assert their own power over the whole of England. From the reign of Henry II onwards, kings began to resurrect the county courts at the expense of the baronial, and to link the former strongly to the central government. Local men again were used to run local affairs as they had been before the conquest. But whereas before the conquest these local communities had considered themselves virtually independent, in the thirteenth century their officials were acting in obedience to instructions from the king, and little was done in local government without the agreement of the central government. The crown began to impose on these shire courts an ever-growing number of duties, and from the middle of the twelfth century a new class of local administrators began to appear – that of the knights of the shires.

Who were these knights of the shires? Generally they were landowners of fair income and independence. Often they were descended from younger sons of tenants-in-chief, and sometimes they were minor direct tenants of the king's, not important enough to rank among the great barons. These men lived on their estates, and on their shoulders lay a great many of the duties of local government.

The knights of the shires had varied responsibilities. They co-operated in ruling the shires with royal officials sent from Westminster. They served as sheriffs and coroners, and often as justices on special commissions to

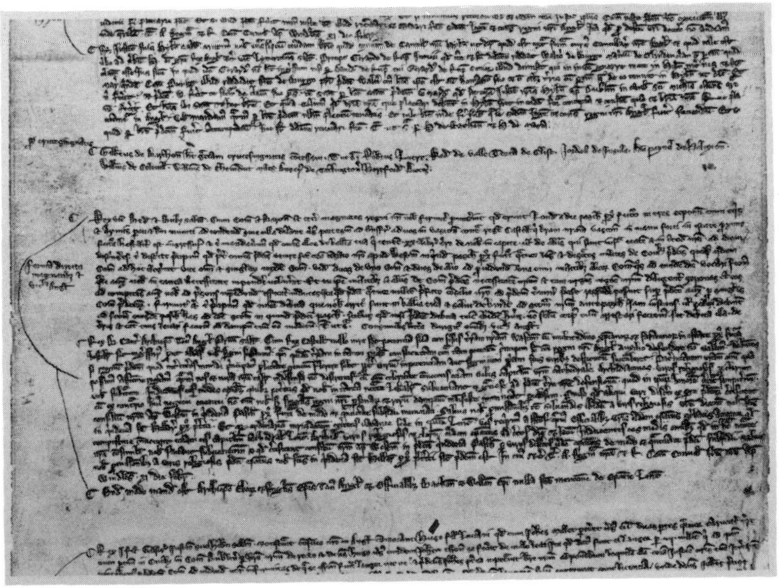

This document of 11 *February* 1254 *shows the enrolment of a writ to the sheriff of Bedfordshire and Buckinghamshire. It tells how the earls, barons and other magnates have promised to go to the king's aid in Gascony and orders the sheriff to see to the appearance before the council at Westminster at Easter of two "lawful and discreet knights from each county . . . specially elected by the county in the name of one and all . . . to consider, together with the knights of the other counties whom we have summoned for the same day, what aid they are willing to grant us in our great need."*

relieve the over-worked royal judges. They sat on committees, acted as jurymen, assessed taxes and investigated local abuses and grievances. For all this they were unpaid, their chief reward being the growing importance of their positions in the shires.

In the course of their duties the knights of the shires sometimes had to travel to Westminster. At first they were merely responsible messengers from their shires, carrying records of cases tried in the local courts to the central king's court. Then we find them carrying reports of an administrative nature to the king's council. For example, in 1226 four knights were chosen from each of eight counties to report to the council on the conduct of sheriffs in their counties, and this happened again in 1227 and 1258. In 1254 the knights were given further responsibilities. The king needed money for his war in Gascony, and decided to try and raise it in England from those who were not coming to fight. It was suggested that if the consent of each county could be obtained in advance and this made known to his council his chances of success would be far greater. Thus each sheriff was ordered to discuss the king's need in his county court, and the knights were then to carry the resulting decision to the small council at Westminster. Here they were acting as delegates from their shires to report a decision reached by their associates, but they had not yet been summoned to a meeting of the Great Council, or parliament.

The knights were thus not unfamiliar with Westminster and had established contacts with the king's small council. However before 1260 they had never been summoned to discuss public affairs as individuals in their own right, but only to report decisions already reached by their shires. In 1261 the next step was taken. At the command of his barons, Henry III ordered each sheriff to send three knights to meet the Great Council at Windsor to discuss affairs of the realm. With king and barons they were to take part in a general discussion of policy. It was not far from this to Simon de Montfort's parliaments of 1264 and 1265.

IX

The Knights in Parliament

THROUGH their work in the shires and their contacts with the central government, the knights were becoming a politically educated class. They were growing more aware of many abuses in local government, and they were beginning to voice their grievances. Probably many of them were educated at the universities, and would there have come into contact with the friars, who were urging reform and the creation of a more just society. The knights were in close contact with the smaller tenants of the shires, often suffering under the yoke of a stern lord. As the barons pressed for reform in the central government, so the knights wished for changes further down the social scale. They wanted to see an end put to unjust administrative practices, and greedy royal officials to be dismissed from office; they wanted widows and minors to be protected from grasping overlords, and generally for the complaints of the lesser freeholders to be investigated, even those of the poorest and most obscure of them. In 1259 their opinions became very audible.

In 1258, as we have already seen in chapter six, Simon de Montfort and the barons had gathered at Oxford, and King Henry had agreed reluctantly to accept their scheme for reform, the Provisions of Oxford. In these reforms the barons had not merely been thinking of improving their own positions; they had touched on grievances that affected all sections of the nation. "We wish," their spokesman had declared some years before, "to keep in mind the common welfare of the realm and not to burden the poor." To this end four knights in every shire had been appointed to draw up lists of grievances and unjust practices. This was about as far as the barons' noble intentions went. When they realized that redress of local grievances would often mean a loss of profits for themselves as landlords, they soon became less enthusiastic. Forgetting their high ideals, many concentrated on bettering their own positions, and these were the men who were to quarrel later with Simon de Montfort and finally to desert his cause.

When it became obvious that the barons were not going to carry out all their good intentions to redress grievances of rich and poor alike, the knights banded together and addressed a protest to Prince Edward, King Henry's son and heir. Edward, realizing how important their support might be to him when he became king, agreed to help their cause, and in 1259 reforms called the Provisions of Westminster were enacted, and these did much to make the lives of the poorer small-holders less hard.

Simon de Montfort had supported the knights' claims in 1259, and had not betrayed his oath to hold to the Provisions of Oxford as so many of his fellow barons had done. Because of this, the mass of lesser landowners and knights in their turn supported his cause. In June, 1264, a parliament was called together, and many magnates and bishops were summoned to attend. Each county was ordered to send four "discreet and loyal knights chosen by them" to represent "the whole community of the realm of England". It was the same story in Simon's famous parliament, which met at Westminster in January, 1265, and of which we shall hear more later. This time two knights were to come from every shire.

As in earlier parliaments, there was probably no idea

of letting the knights air their own opinions, or play an active part in the discussions. They were there as witnesses, to see justice done and to spread the word throughout England that it had been done. They were also there to pledge their shires to pay a share of the taxes that the government would demand. Simon de Montfort valued efficient government very highly, and he knew that government by consent of a large part of the nation led most surely to this.

X

The Boroughs Advance

ONE OF the great fairs or markets in medieval England was held in the town of Stourbridge near Cambridge. Every year in early September this fair was opened and for the following three weeks a crowd of wooden booths would offer for sale everything that visitors from the neighbouring countryside might wish for: there were opportunities to buy soap and garlic, salt and honey, coal and linen, cheese and almonds. Foreign merchants mingled with English tradesmen in showing their wares, and, because a fair was a time for enjoyment as well as for exchange of merchandise, there were horse-races, wrestling matches, gambling, rope-dancers and a maypole. It was a time for town and country folk to meet each other and to mingle with traders from far and near – a time for discussion and gossip, the exchange of ideas as well as goods, a time when the town was in its rightful rôle as the heart of a thriving community.

All over England in the thirteenth century, these fairs took place, and some, like Stourbridge, acquired a high reputation for the quality of their goods and the extent of their festivities. They give us a very bright picture of the growing prosperity and vitality of most English towns. Each had several industries, and contact with foreign merchants meant the spread of new ideas, whilst the growth of trade made many of them prosperous

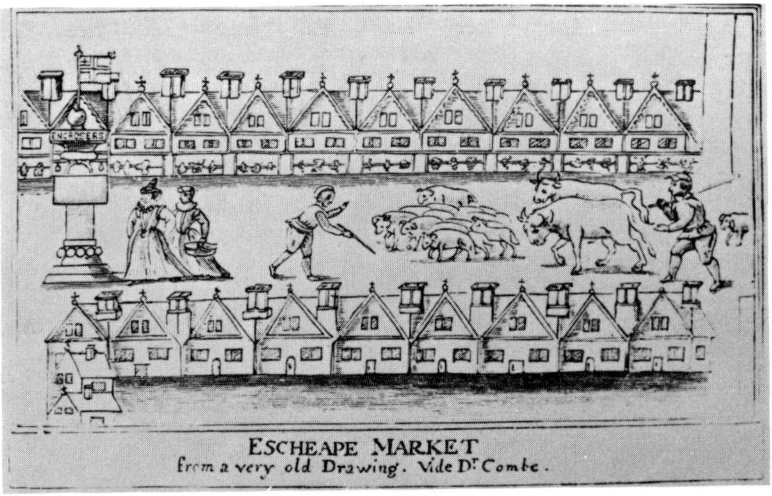

A medieval market.

centres and helped to give them new importance in the political life of their nation.

How had these towns grown up in a land of farming communities, whose interests lay in the soil rather than the High Street? The Anglo-Saxons, fighting the Danish invaders in the ninth century, had fortified the older trading centres, calling them *burhs* or boroughs. It was not size or wealth that made a borough town, but solely the king's will. He created them in areas where he wanted centres of defence against the Danes, and they grew under his royal protection and control. Their markets and mints were privileges granted and protected by the king.

In Saxon times every shire had at least one borough town. The Saxon kings encouraged their growth and wished to make the men who dwelt in them proud of their status. All who lived in a borough were free men, paying a money rent for their land, with none of the duties and obligations of the villein attached; a serf who escaped to a town in the middle ages could claim to be regarded as a free man if he was accepted there, and lived unchallenged within its walls for a year and a day. Londoners were granted even higher status than that of being merely free men. Their leading citizens were recognized as barons and even claimed the right to play an important part in the making of a king. The great men of the Cinque Ports also claimed the title of barons. They had the responsibility of finding ships and sailors when the king wanted them.

After 1066, many boroughs were founded by local magnates, anxious to impress their authority on the surrounding countryside. A new town was generally given a charter by its lord, in which the burgesses' privileges were set out. Later on the king sometimes

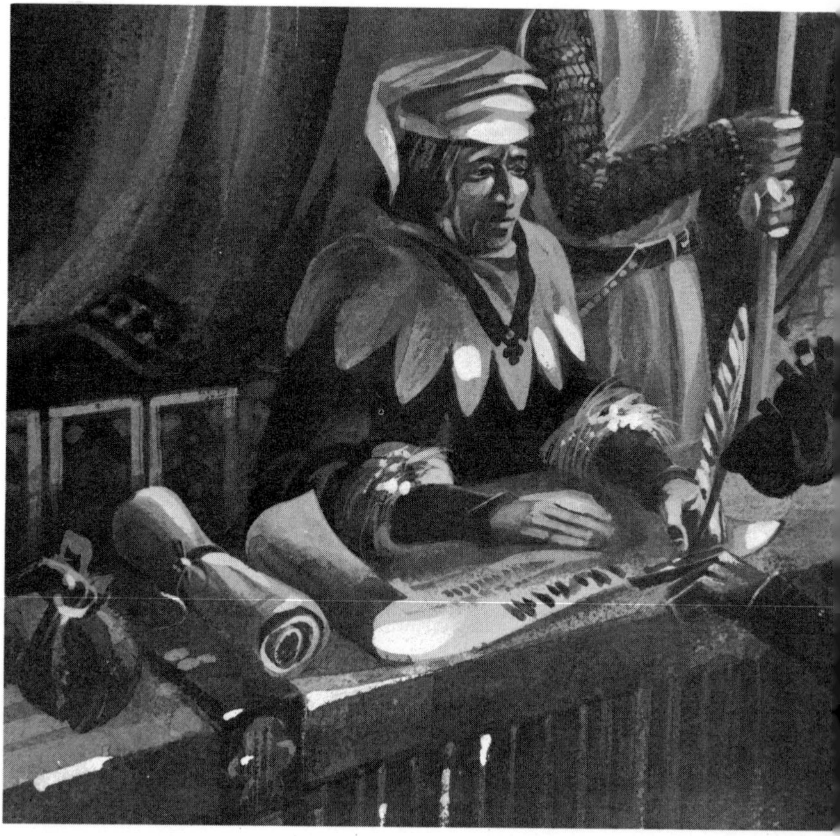

granted more privileges, also by charter.

Most boroughs were closely connected to their shires. Although they had their own town-courts, the sheriff collected all rents and dues owed to the king in the town, just as he did in the shire. To him or to the local magnate went also the profits of the town-court. Many burgesses, conscious of their positions and importance, wished to be free of this interference from sheriff and baron. They wanted to be free to pay their own taxes to the exchequer. Richard I sold many charters of freedom to boroughs all over England, because he was always in need of money for his Crusades, and this continued under his brother, King John. By 1216 only

those towns who could not afford to buy their privileges were still not independent of the sheriff and his county officials.

As the towns became more prosperous, and as merchants began to travel between them more easily, so in each town associations of traders began to grow up. These were called the merchant gilds. Their members came from every trade in the town, and their aims were to protect their own interests against those of strangers, to fix wages, and to prevent the use of false weights and measures. There was a gild court, which could impose fines against members of the gild, or prevent men from following their trade for one year. These self-governing associations trained men for the part they were later to play in national politics. As trading horizons widened, so they became more aware of their nationality, and of political issues that might affect all Englishmen.

When the boroughs began to gain independence and the right to govern their own affairs, so the leaders of these gilds became the leaders of the whole community. The administrators of a borough were too often chosen from a small number of prominent families, who had become important through their positions in the gilds. At first the smaller burgesses in the towns did not question the justice of this; however in the thirteenth century they were becoming more conscious of their privileges and growing importance. Just as the knights of the shires were rebelling against the power of their lords, so many burgesses reacted against their borough governments, and both knights and burgesses would come to regard Simon de Montfort as their champion.

XI

The Boroughs Raise their Voices

To the towns came foreign merchants and pilgrims, travellers passing through and young men from the countryside seeking apprenticeship to a trade; there too came the friars, to heal the sick and tend the poor and aged, and to preach in the market square, not only on Christian subjects, but also on the need for just government and on the responsibility of the ruler towards his people. These ideas appealed to the more active and ambitious burgesses, who began to look more critically at the government of their country by Henry III, and also of their town by the merchant gild.

These townsmen found plenty to complain about. They saw their hard-won wealth drained away by the king's demands. As their prosperity had increased, so had his needs. Money had to be found for his wars in Gascony and Poitou, for his extravagance at home and for his schemes in Sicily. The boroughs were an obvious source of riches, and again and again Henry demanded huge taxes and "gifts". The burgesses felt that their money was being dissipated on royal favourites and court ceremonial, or on projects abroad that would bring them no benefit and might even disrupt foreign trade.

London especially was a turbulent city full of unrest, where discontent might flare up into rioting and disorder at any moment. The citizens of London were proud of their city and jealous of their independence. They resented the king's power to demand money from them. There was an old saying: "Come what may, the Londoners should have no king but their mayor." The mayor of London had taken his place at Runnymede among the twenty-five greatest magnates of the realm. He ruled the city with the help of two sheriffs and a court of aldermen representing every area or ward of the capital. Yet, as in the country towns, the government of London had passed into the hands of a few of the wealthier merchant families, and the smaller burgesses resented this and longed to gain control. In Simon de Montfort they were to see a leader who would restore the government of the city to representatives of the whole body of citizens, and who would free them from the greedy demands of Henry III. They would flock to his side deposing their mayor and aldermen, and putting new men in their places. Very often the old borough governments had supported King Henry, but these new men would want to see Earl Simon in power and the Provisions of Oxford put into practice.

With all this enthusiastic support for his cause from the townspeople, it is not surprising that Simon de Montfort did not forget them when he called together his parliament in January, 1265, of which we shall hear more later. For the first time writs were sent to the boroughs, ordering each to send two representatives to the parliament. At that time Simon needed to show his powerful position to the king and royalists by gathering together an impressive body of supporters at this parliament. He knew that he could rely on the burgesses just as he could rely on the knights of the shires. Like the latter, the burgesses were not to play any large part in this parliament. They were there as witnesses of what was agreed, so that they could report to their towns the decisions reached. It was probably not the first time that many of them had been to Westminster; like the shires, the boroughs had for some time been sending

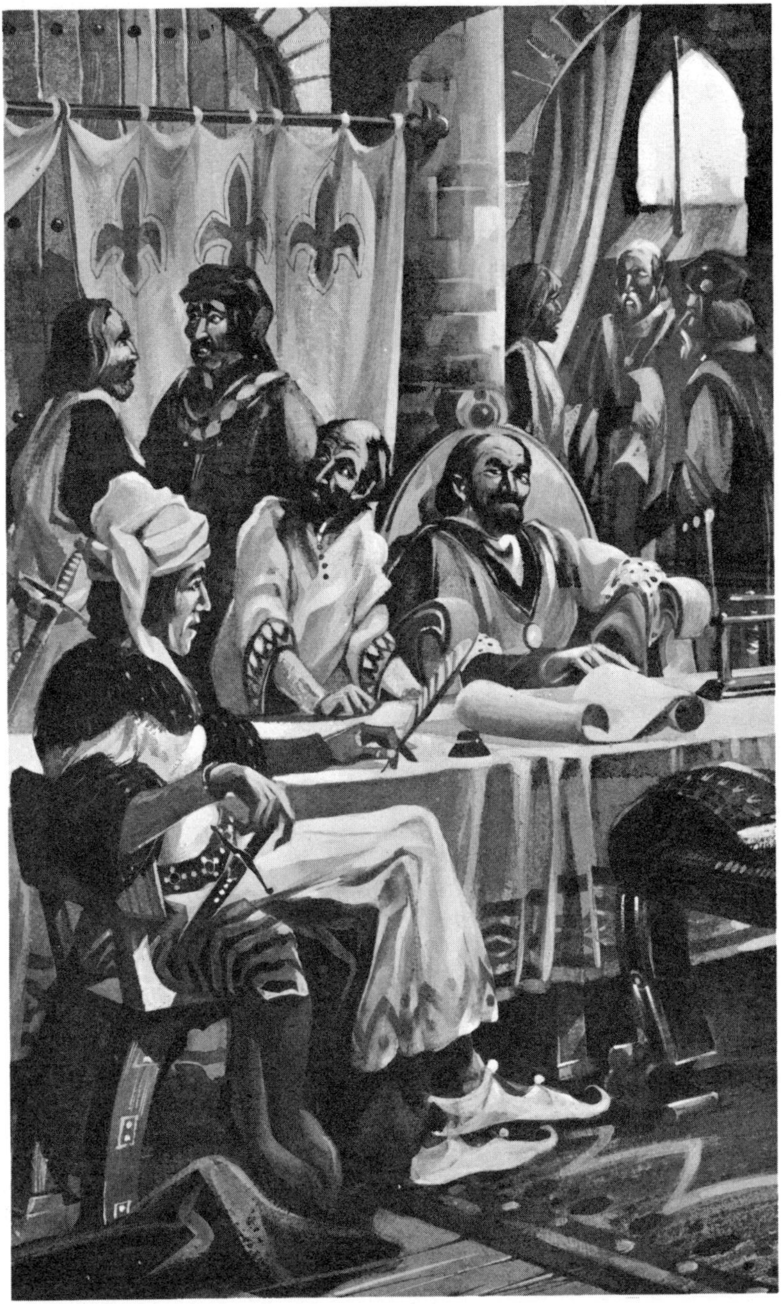

delegates to the central government to report on administrative matters and to carry decisions made there back to their towns. They had also been sending representatives to the shire courts when the royal justices appeared on their circuits, so they were used to the idea of electing a few townspeople to represent the rest. Now for the first time, they joined with the knights in attending a great council held to discuss national policy. Although probably none of them spoke during any of the meetings, the important point is that they were members of the parliament.

It was probably not a very popular move of Simon's to ask the boroughs to send delegates to his 1265 parliament. For many of them it was a long journey to London, and the borough had to pay all the expenses. Then there was accommodation to find in London, and who knew how long they might have to stay? When it became quite accepted that the boroughs should be represented in parliament, some towns petitioned the king for the privilege of not having to send members. The townsfolk did not really want a part in the government of England; they wanted to be sure of their independence, and that their grievances would be remedied. With so much expansion of trade and growth of opportunity, they wanted to be free to develop their resources, without interference from the king or his government.

XII

The Adventurer from Montfort l'Amaury

FOR THE beginning of Simon de Montfort's personal story we must go back to the charming little old French town that bears his name – Montfort l'Amaury. It lies on high ground between the valleys of the river Eure and the river Seine, in the south-east corner of Normandy, midway between Paris and Chartres. Close to the little town is a ruined castle high upon a grassy mound. This was the natural fortress, the "strong mount" that attracted the attention of the first of the family who took its name from the stronghold and of which Simon de Montfort was the descendant.

It would have been hard, at the beginning of the thirteenth century, to find a family of greater force of character and of greater pretensions than that of de Montfort. They flash in and out of the history of those times, making brilliant and wealthy marriages and acquiring noble properties. Closely connected with England as well as with France, they could claim an equality of birth with the English kings themselves.

The grandfather of our Simon was the third count of Montfort and was known as Simon the Bald. He was descended from a king of France and, by his marriage to the heiress of Robert Fitzparnel, earl of Leicester, was able to hand down to his son this earldom, large English estates, and the dignity of high steward of England.

The ruined castle of Montfort l'Amaury, the home of the de Montfort family in France.

Petronilla, the widow of Robert Fitzparnel, was the noble lady who furnished the church of Leicester with a curious piece of fancy work, a rope made of her own hair with which to hang up the lamp in the choir.

The father of our Simon, the fourth count of Montfort, accordingly became earl of Leicester in due course, but during troubles with King John in 1207 his estates were seized and he was banished from England. He must have had some bold and powerful supporters, for King John was afterwards startled by a report (which turned out to be false) that the barons had elected the count to be king in his place.

A good soldier and remarkable for his stature and strength, this count had the opportunity, during his exile from England, of making his name known, hated and feared throughout southern Europe by his barbarous crusade against the Albigenses. The cruelties practised are well known, but the widely spread fanaticism of the period and the merit of exterminating heretics is reflected in one historian's appraisal of the count. After telling of the count's order, at the capture of the castle of Brom, that the noses of a hundred of the garrison be cut off and their eyes plucked out he refers to him as "the mildest of men".

There is reason to believe however that service under him was unpopular with his troops and repugnant to their common feelings of humanity, for the count, in a letter to the pope, stated that "he had been obliged to hire soldiers to remain with him at a greater price than in other wars, so that he could scarcely keep them unless rewarded by double pay".

This zealot has been compared to Oliver Cromwell, for the count was well fitted for a holy war and superior to the meaner superstitions of his time. When his wife came to him greatly alarmed at having dreamed of blood flowing from her arms, he discounted her fears.

"Do you think we follow dreams and auguries like the Spaniards?" he asked. "Even if you had dreamed that

A de Montfort chateau in the south of France.

I was to die in this war I should go forward so much the bolder and freer, in order to reprove such folly."

The countess was indeed not unlikely to have such dreams of blood; for she shared all her husband's perils of war, at one time leading a reinforcement of 15,000 soldiers to him, at another enduring with her children the miseries of a besieged city.

In the beautiful French country around Albi there are still to be seen several noble castles that this savage de Montfort either occupied for a time or besieged during this cruel crusade. All his power and fame however came to a sudden stop in 1218. While besieging the city of Toulouse he was struck on the head by a stone pitched from a mangonel used to defend the city and so died ingloriously.

From this fierce and noble parentage was born the Simon de Montfort of our English history. He was the youngest of four sons and a youth of about eighteen years at the time of his father's death.

The eldest son, Amaury, inherited all the French lands and possessions of his warlike father, whilst Simon, the youngest, was left with no prospects. Of his early life and education we know nothing, but since Amaury's teacher was Master Nicholas, one of the best mathematicians of his day according to the famous Franciscan friar Roger Bacon, his schooling was presumably not neglected. He was well skilled in the use of arms and, like his father, tall and handsome.

Now that a new king, Henry III, sat upon England's throne and there was peace with France, the de Montfort family's hopes of regaining their English earldom were renewed. The young Simon, with his elder brother's agreement, determined to go to England and try to claim the inheritance that had once been his father's. He would also try to see what he could achieve in the way of a rich marriage.

XIII

The Adventurer Arrives to Seek his Fortune

SIMON DE MONTFORT did not find it all plain sailing when he embarked on his first efforts to take his place among Englishmen. He had first to encounter the growing opposition of the English nobility to foreigners, which seems to have been successful in so far as it kept him for some years from the title, as well as the advantages, of his earldom. Neither did King Henry do anything more for him than promise him an annual payment of 400 marks until he received the earldom.

Here in Simon's own words is his request to the king for his inheritance:

First, our Lord the king says he has done me great goodness in that he took me for his man, because I was not the eldest. And so that one may know what the goodness was, my brother Amaury released to me all the right that he had in our father's inheritance in England, if I could secure it, in the same manner that I released to him the heritage which I had in France. And I went to England and prayed my lord the king that he would restore to me my father's inheritance. And he answered that he could not, because he had given it to the earl of Chester and his heirs by his charter. Upon this I returned without finding grace. The following year my lord the king crossed to Brittany and with him the earl of Chester who held my inheritance. And I went to the earl at the castle of St James de Beuvon which he held. There

I prayed him that I could find his grace to have my inheritance and he, graciously, agreed, and in the following August took me with him to England and asked the king to receive my homage for the inheritance of my father, to which, as he said, I had greater right than he, and all the gifts which the king had given him in this he renounced, and so he received my homage.

The official letters of August 1231 do indeed show that Earl Ranulf of Chester took Simon back to England with him then and pleaded with the king to accept him as the rightful heir to the earldom of Leicester. On 13 August of that year the king ordered the sheriffs of Leicester, Hampshire, Dorset and Wiltshire to give full possession of the earldom lands to Simon, since the king had received his homage for the honour of Leicester which belonged to him by hereditary right. From this time onwards the Leicester lands and revenues belonged to Simon, though the king was not to invest him formally with the title for another eight years.

Being an attractive and ambitious young man, "a gentleman of choice blood, education and features", Simon de Montfort was not slow in rising to favour at the court of King Henry III, who was always favourably disposed towards foreigners. But his difficulties were by no means over. The meagre income from his estates was not enough to support the state of an earl and he was looked upon by the wealthy English nobles as little more than a penniless adventurer. It is not to be wondered at that he spent much of his time abroad, as many another needy gentleman has had to do. Of this period of his life we know but little. He does not seem to have been employed on any service of state for the first few years. It was during this time that he was foiled in two attempts to better his fortunes by marriage. Fully sensible of the maxim of a quaint author of his times that "a woman who has lands of her own is much the most desirable" (a maxim not out of date though 600 years old) he had twice sought the hand in marriage of widowed ladies of princely blood. But in each case his hopes were dashed by the opposition of the French king, jealous of his connection with England.

The marriage of King Henry III in 1236 brought him back to England and we find him for the first time in his office of lord high steward of England at the coronation feast of the new queen.

King Henry, in love for the first time at the age of twenty-nine, married the beautiful Eleanor, one of the four queenly daughters of Raymond, count of Provence. She was only fourteen years old and had no dowry, but she was passionate and high-spirited and devoted to her husband. The marriage took place at Canterbury on

4 January, 1236, soon after the royal bride had landed at Dover, and preparations of the most extraordinary magnificence were made for the approaching coronation. We read that the good citizens of London in their zeal to do honour to their new queen set about the task of cleansing their streets from mud and all other offensive accumulations which rendered the way almost impassable. A mounted procession of citizens who claimed the office of cellarers to the king accompanied the royal couple from the Tower of London where they were lodged. Numbering 360, they were clothed in long garments embroidered with gold and silk in various

colours and their steeds were arrayed in fine trappings with shining bits and new saddles. Each citizen carried a gold or silver cup in his hand for the royal use and the king's trumpeters sounded before them. They rode in to the royal banquet and served the king and queen and all the noble company with wine, according to old custom and their duty.

It was the duty of Simon de Montfort, as lord high steward, to look after the royal kitchen and to arrange the banquet. During the feast and dressed in his robes of office his was the privilege of bringing the king a basin of water in which to wash his hands. When the festivities were over the steward had, according to custom, to give his ceremonial robes to the master cook.

Alms were bounteously distributed to the poor, for King Henry, with all his faults and love of luxury, was one of the most charitable of men. The expenses however of all this ceremonial and of the sumptuous banquet were enormous, and very soon murmurings of discontent at the extravagance of the king and his new young queen began to be heard.

XIV

A Princess for his Bride

SIMON DE MONTFORT had been steadily growing in the royal favour since the time he had been granted the Leicester lands. The king had become fond of him and now he was one of his most trusted counsellors. Attractive and ambitious he undoubtedly was and now a dazzling prize was to come within his grasp, for he won the hand and the heart of another Eleanor, a princess and the beautiful widowed sister of the king.

When she was quite a child Princess Eleanor had been married to William, earl of Pembroke, son of the old marshal who had done so much for England in the early days of King Henry's reign. But William had died young and his death had left Eleanor very wealthy. She had been left in the care of a gentlewoman called Cicely de Sandford, who was also a widow and acted as governess and teacher of morals to her young charge. She is described as being "noble in blood, but more noble in manners, very learned, eloquent and courteous".

Being extremely pious as well, Cicely decided to take a vow of chastity before the archbishop of Canterbury and influenced her charge to do likewise. The governess and the young girl both took a vow that they would never marry and accepted the ring that marked them as wedded to Christ. They did not take the veil which usually marked the solemn sealing of the pact, but they began to dress in russet, the coarse homespun material usually worn by peasants and given as alms by the rich to the poor.

This vow, although not complete, was to cause a great deal of trouble to Eleanor later on. When she had got over her husband's death and began to outgrow the influence of her governess she began to long for fine dresses and to marry again. The determined governess, however, remained faithful to her vow to the end. As she lay dying, her confessor, a friar, tried to take the ring off her finger; but the sick woman revived enough to warn him that "living or dead, no one could take away her ring, which she would carry to the tribunal of God in testimony of her inviolable chastity". So saying, she curved her fingers round it so that her servants could not slip it off, and died.

King Henry was very good to his sister Eleanor and she spent much of her time at court. She also travelled about a good deal from place to place with her retinue. Her brother the king would order his officials to provide lodgings for her wherever she wanted to go, and deer from the royal forests were sent to her. When she asked him for a separate establishment of her own, suitable to her position, he gave her the new castle and manor of Odiham. This was a valuable stronghold and also very convenient, for it was situated between Windsor and Winchester, two of the king's favourite residences.

It was not long before the Princess Eleanor fell in love with the handsome young Simon de Montfort, who had been wooing her so earnestly. In spite of the archbishop's warning that Eleanor was promised to the church, the king looked with the greatest favour upon the match between his sister and his friend.

On the day after the Feast of the Epiphany in January, 1238, in the small private chapel that led out of his painted chamber, the king himself placed his sister's hand in that of his friend and favourite, and we read that Simon

The seal of Eleanor de Montfort.

"took her with pleasure because of the love he felt for the princess, for her beauty and illustrious birth".

What were the reasons for the secrecy and haste of this wedding? Was the king trying to assert his authority over his barons and the church by giving his sister in marriage to his favourite? Was this a fait accompli which they might deplore but could not change?

Whatever the reasons, this arbitrary conduct raised a storm among the barons. Had not the king on many occasions sworn not to take any important decision without asking their advice? Had they not a lawful right of control over the marriage of the most noble heiress in the kingdom? The clerics, especially the friars and monks, were shocked at Eleanor's remarriage because it broke her vow of celibacy. The barons, already jealous of the foreigner Simon's popularity with the king, were furious that by this marriage he should have risen to such a high position. The citizens of London, who, twenty years later, were to be Simon's

staunchest allies, now joined in the general outcry against him. Richard of Cornwall, the king's brother, was particularly enraged that he had not been consulted, for Simon had been his close friend. The whole kingdom was in an uproar and the king himself overwhelmed and confused, in fear of a revolt.

But by his submissive bearing, by promises and gifts, and perhaps by his personal charm and his wife's intercessions, Simon won over Richard of Cornwall, and some of the barons, and the storm died down.

The opposition of the church, however, remained as strong as ever, and Simon set off for Rome, armed with letters from the king to the pope asking for dispensation of Eleanor's former vow of celibacy. He took with him as much gold as he could muster to speed the slowly turning wheels of papal justice.

Simon's plea to the pope was eventually granted and he returned to England in the autumn with the dispensation that was essential to make the marriage legal. A chronicler of the times tells us that he was received with rejoicing by the king and his household. The clouds of disapproval had rolled away, but Simon did not linger long at court. He hastened north to the royal castle of Kenilworth where his wife had remained all the time he was away. The king had made sure that his sister received the best in food and wine during this time, for the ancient rolls are full of details of gifts of deer and wine and, on one occasion "six tuns of better Wine".

28 November saw the birth of Simon's and Eleanor's first son, an occasion for much rejoicing. King Henry stood godfather to the child and allowed him to be named Henry after him.

XV

The King's Wrath Falls upon Simon and his Wife

THE KING and queen celebrated the following Christmas at Winchester. Simon was back in his place once more as one of the king's most trusted counsellors and his wife was at his side.

The king's Christmas present to his sister that year was a magnificent one. A length of the rich baudekin cloth for a robe and tunic with miniver fur to trim and line it, also a quilt of the same material for her bed and a coverlet of grey fur lined with scarlet cloth. It was during these joyful Christmas festivities that the king decided to invest Simon with his proper title as the earl of Leicester. This took place on the feast of Candlemas early in the New Year in the presence of the assembled barons.

At peace in his home at Odiham Simon's prospects must have seemed bright indeed, for he had fulfilled his ambitions in the country he had adopted for his own. He had achieved the earldom of Leicester; he had married the king's sister, who was greatly his superior in wealth and prestige; he stood high in favour with the king, and he had a son and heir of his own.

Nevertheless things were not as perfect as they seemed. No one could rely upon the fickle king's favour for long, and already the seeds of the conflict that was to come between earl and king had been sown.

In June 1239 a son was born to King Henry and Queen Eleanor and he was named Edward (afterwards Edward I). Simon stood godfather to the child and acted as high steward at his baptism. The baby was lifted from the font by three bishops and three earls and one of these was Simon de Montfort. This was regarded as a mark of great favour.

The king seized the opportunity to extort money from those to whom he announced the happy event of the birth of his heir and successor to the throne. If the presents he received did not satisfy him he sent the messengers back for more, so that people remarked "God gave us this child, but my lord the king sells him to us."

Each noble was expected to make a costly gift to celebrate the happy event, for King Henry's finances were very low at this time and the birth of an heir was made an excuse for filling up the royal coffers.

The next event was the grand festival the queen gave on the occasion of her solemn churching in Westminster abbey. The king summoned all the great ladies of the land to attend her to church and Simon brought his wife to perform this duty. To their horror the king suddenly burst into a wild storm of rage against them both, calling Simon an excommunicated man, forbidding either of them to enter the abbey, and ordering his attendants to turn them out of the palace. Simon tried to remonstrate but the king would not hear him and drove them both from his presence. Astonished and deeply hurt by these reproaches, the earl and countess retired across the river to the palace of the late bishop of Winchester, where they hoped to lodge. But no sooner had they arrived there than the king sent messengers to eject them. Whereupon they returned to the palace and made one more attempt to appease the angry king, but in vain. He continued to rage against them in the most violent manner and with much abusive language. One account says he was so angry that he wanted to have Simon imprisoned in the Tower immediately, but was persuaded by his brother,

Richard of Cornwall, to see reason. Did this quarrel arise from personal antipathy or was it significant of the deeper struggle for power that was later to evolve between these two men? It seems most likely that the prime cause was money. The control of Eleanor de Montfort's dowry was a constant source of dissension, and the king accused Simon of having bribed the pope to secure the dispensation for his marriage.

Finally, we are told, the earl, red with shame and anger, withdrew, and as soon as night fell he and his wife and their small household took a little boat down the Thames and fled across the Channel to France.

There they stayed for some time while the king's anger cooled. It was during this time that Simon took the cross and went off on crusade to the Holy Land. Leaving his wife in a castle at Brindisi he joined Richard of Cornwall in Syria, where he made a great impression upon the barons of the Latin kingdom of Jerusalem. In such high esteem was he held that some of them petitioned the emperor, Frederick II, to appoint him governor of the kingdom. Nothing came of this, but it was nevertheless significant of his reputation as a warrior and leader of men.

The year 1242 saw Simon back in England again, being welcomed with all honour by the king. All quarrels seemed forgotten and so fully did the sun of the royal favour now shine upon him that he was one of the twelve who, at the important council of that year, were commissioned by the king to sort out the confusion of his finances. During this council the king met from the barons the most determined opposition to his demands for money and had to submit to a sound rating for his wastefulness and extravagance.

During this time King Henry was persuaded by his mother, the turbulent Isabella, to renew the struggle against France for the recovery of Poitou. Isabella's husband, the count de la Marche, promised to find the men if the English would provide the money. King

Henry, with his usual rashness and shortsighted ambition, entered on this expedition with a light heart. Despite opposition from the barons and unable to raise the money from them en masse he managed to extort it from them singly.

An old song describes how, at the assembly in London at which the king proposed the expedition, "not a baron, from best to worst, will move"; afterwards, however, the earls of Gloucester and Winchester support the king, outdoing him in boasting. Upon which Simon de Montfort starts to his feet with anger in his face and advises the king to let the matter drop, for "the Frenchman is no lamb" and will defend himself bravely:

"*De Montfort starts up, looking grim to scoff,*
When the boasting king he hears.
By the lamb of God, leave this meddling off,
For France is no lamb for your shears.
Why how now Simon! le Bigot cries out,
Do you set the king down for a fool or a lout?"

Thereupon a quarrel ensues between Simon and the king, who is indignant at Simon's freedom of speech. But finally the king is appeased and there is an end to the dispute.

The expedition undertaken so lightly ended in miserable failure. The count de la Marche proved a broken reed. Deserted by him, the English suffered a severe defeat at the battle of Saintes, but the earls of Leicester, Salisbury and Norfolk, with a few other great barons, were able to save the army from destruction and the country from the penalty of a royal ransom.

During this campaign Simon de Montfort's temper was tried to the utmost by the stupidity of the king and he made a remark that Henry was to remember twenty years later. It would be better, he said, if the king were taken and kept in one place, as Charles the Foolish had been, and added that there were houses barred with iron at Windsor which would be good places for this purpose.

Although Simon's temper was violent his tactics were right and finally the king agreed to abandon the campaign and they all retreated to Bordeaux.

The queen joined her husband at Bordeaux and they then resolved to spend a merry winter there, where they amused themselves with as much feasting and pageantry as if King Henry had won the most splendid victory instead of being considerably impoverished by the failure of the campaign and the loss of some of his treasure, including his moveable chapel royal with all its rich plate. Many of the barons and nobles left for England, disgusted at the failure of the campaign and the idle frivolities in which the king wasted time and money in Bordeaux, but Simon de Montfort remained at the royal side. Conditions in France were very bad and the king requested food supplies, clothes and money to be sent out from England. There the English were enduring an unusually wet winter and November was marked by terrific thunderstorms; the heavy rain caused the Thames to flood "so that they could swim boats in the great hall of Westminster".

After the winter the king and queen and their court all returned to England for the marriage of the queen's youngest sister, Sanchia, to the king's brother, Richard of Cornwall. After all the extravagant festivities of the wedding, which the king enjoyed to the full, he was in such a good mood that he bestowed several more tokens of his favour upon Simon de Montfort. Doubtless the gallant part that Simon had played during the fighting in France also increased the high favour in which he stood with the king at this time. He bestowed upon him the custody of the castle of Kenilworth, greatest of all the midland fortresses. Originally it had been under royal control and had been strengthened and considerably improved. In the castles of Kenilworth and of Odiham, which had been given to Simon's wife Eleanor before her marriage, the earl and countess of Leicester now possessed two of the strongest fortresses in England.

Kenilworth castle.

XVI

The King's Misrule

THE YEARS passed under the misrule of King Henry, and the discontentment of all classes of people grew more rather than less. The campaign in France had brought the king nothing but debts and he was permanently in need of money. His extravagance and the growing unpopularity of the queen, coupled with the unruly behaviour of their many foreign relations whom they had raised to high places in court and state, exasperated barons and people alike. The insatiable demands of the pope for more and more money out of England added to their burden, while the lawless state of the country became so bad that in Hampshire no jury dared to convict any plunderer. The chronicler Matthew Paris wrote that "King Henry himself complained that when he was travelling with the queen through that country their luggage was robbed, their wine drunk and themselves insulted by the lawless rabble." The king could find no judge who would undertake to see that justice was done and was forced to sit on the bench himself in Winchester castle. While thus presiding there he had occasion to summon Lord Clifford to answer for some malefaction. When the disagreeable writ was presented to him Lord Clifford forced the king's messenger to eat the document, parchment, wax seal and all. The king, however, punished this lord with spirit and with courage.

During these troubled years Simon de Montfort was mostly at his home in Kenilworth castle with his young family growing up around him. His five sons were sometimes at court and acted as playfellows to their royal cousins, but mostly they were under the tutorship of the great and saintly Robert Grosseteste, the learned bishop of Lincoln. This brilliant and remarkable man was to become one of Simon and Eleanor's greatest friends and his influence upon Simon's character was considerable.

Born a poor peasant in Suffolk, of the meanest parentage, Robert Grosseteste (this name means Greathead and was given to him because of the large size of his head) received his education in some unknown way and worked until he became a noted teacher at Oxford and afterwards in Paris. He lectured on all the chief Greek and Latin authors and wrote 200 books and a number of poems in Latin and French. He was a great lover of minstrelsy and kept his harp in a room adjoining his study. But while he was a great scholar he was also a practical man and an ardent reformer, struggling to combat the many evils in the church and the exactions of the king and the pope. He was also exceedingly generous and when chosen as bishop of Lincoln showed his gratitude for the benefits of education by maintaining out of his own purse a number of poor students at Oxford university. He wrote to Pope Innocent exposing the enormities that were being practised in England by the foreign clergy, and it is said that the pope actually blushed and owned that he had been wrong in appointing incompetent Italians to the English church livings. One good result of this was that when King Henry appointed one of his favourites to be bishop of Chichester, Robert Grosseteste examined him and found him to be so ignorant of theology that he urged the appointment instead of Richard Wych, a good and saintly English churchman, and Pope Innocent not only agreed, but consecrated the new bishop himself. King Henry was so angry at this that he took the whole of the income of the see for himself and poor Bishop Wych was obliged to live for many years at the expense of a poor parish priest whom he repaid for his food and lodging by digging and working in his garden.

Simon and Eleanor de Montfort were so fond of the noble-minded Bishop Grosseteste that on one occasion they even lent him their cook, on the death of his own. The Countess Eleanor, far from being annoyed, said that she would gladly lend her best or most necessary servants to the bishop if he had need of them.

Another of the de Montforts' great friends was the learned Franciscan friar Adam Marsh. He was rector of the Franciscan school at Oxford and was well known as a scholar, theologian and mathematician. He was a great reformer and a respected visitor at court as well as friend and counsellor to many bishops. He was spokesman not only for the Franciscans at Oxford but for the whole university. He wrote many letters, as did Bishop Grosseteste, to Simon and his wife, full of advice and counsel, and it was to the influence of these two good men that Simon de Montfort owed much of the moulding of his character during these years.

It was in the year 1248 that King Henry resolved to send "his beloved brother-in-law and faithful Simon de Montfort" as governor to Gascony. Gascony was the last remnant of that great inheritance in southern France that Henry II had acquired through his wife Eleanor of Aquitaine, and throughout the first half of the thirteenth century it was a source of continual anxiety to the English king. The unsettled conditions in England and the fickle nature of its king had had a bad effect on Gascony, and its governors had been changed twenty times since King Henry had come to the throne. The people were lawless and robber barons greatly troubled the land. Commerce was beginning to suffer – Gascony's export of wine to England, and England's bulky export of grain by ship to Gascony. The rescue of the province demanded the best man that could be sent – soldier, statesman and diplomatist all in one. The king knew the dangers and gave Simon de Montfort extraordinary powers. He promised him a grant of money, which, like most of his promises however, remained unfulfilled; money was borrowed for his first expenses and a large sum was extorted from the Londoners.

With such funds as could be hastily collected and with the royal authority for six years Simon set off. His rule was rigorous and he soon restored order to the troubled province and sent the chief rebel, Gaston, count of Bern, as a prisoner to England. Unfortunately King Henry, who never knew how to choose either a friend or an enemy, took this Gaston into his favour and restored his estates to him, thereby enabling him to repeat his rebellion a few years later.

Simon's years in Gascony continued to be stormy, for the province would not stay quiet for long. Robber-barons rode out by night in bands in the manner of thieves, plundering and pillaging the crops and goods of all the lands that lay in their path. Simon's letters to the king during this time show the difficulty of his position and the uncertainty of support at home. His position was indeed a hard one – a constant lack of money, not enough troops of the right sort, a series of isolated castles to take, secret foes at home and the constant danger of war with France. The weak king threw even more difficulties in his way. Some of the rebels escaped from Gascony and came of their own will to England to beg the king's mercy. Some of these the king sent back to Gascony to be tried, with orders that they were to be treated leniently, thus undermining Simon's work. As supplies of money grew ever shorter Simon began to use his own private fortune in carrying out the king's work and even had his own timber cut down to raise money to continue the struggle against the rebels.

He returned to England sometime during the winter of

1250–1251, arriving worn and travel-stained at his home, with only three attendants. In February 1251 he was with the queen at Windsor, endeavouring to persuade her to use her influence with the king on his behalf. But others had been there before him, and though the king could not resist his appeal when made face to face, the answer shows what had been going on behind his back. He had been accused of severity and injustice, even of treachery, and it is evident that the king more than half believed the reports. But so bravely had Simon fought against the rebels and so vigorously did he deny the charges against him that the king could not resist his appeal.

"By the head of God, Sir Earl," said he "thou hast said the truth and I will not refuse thee aid, since thou has fought so well. But grievous complaints have come up to me how those that came to thee in good faith, thou has thrown into prison and allowed to perish in their bonds."

With this surly acquiescence the earl had to be content. He returned to Gascony and set to work to put down the rebels once more. His expenses were no doubt very great; his friend the friar Adam Marsh had to write to the countess warning her not to increase these by luxury and display in dress and to beware of giving way to licence of tongue lest she should increase her husband's difficulties. On the other hand she should help him in every possible way, to keep him to his engagements, and to restrain him from lavish expenditure.

It was fortunate for Simon that he had good friends who kept him informed on the state of things at home. Adam Marsh wrote him words of comfort in his difficulties, referring him to the example of patience in the Book of Job, and added that the king was well inclined towards him, if it were not for the influence of those about him. Another time he wrote that the king had been much annoyed by certain utterances of Simon's that had come to his ears. The earl is therefore warned to set a watch upon his tongue for "the heart of fools is in their mouths, but the mouth of a wise man is in his heart".

The good friar himself however soon incurred the displeasure of the king by his boldness of speech and therefore could no longer further Simon's business at court. The more valuable to Simon must have been the help of his steadfast friend bishop Grosseteste, in whose care he had left his two eldest sons on his departure for Gascony.

Soon after this Simon must have been much saddened by the news of the death of the good bishop. He was much mourned by all who knew him. His noble ideal which he defended against the king and pope alike was that the vast power of the church must be exercised only for the glory of God; no taint of earthly motives must corrupt that dignity which is so high above the earth. His long friendship with Simon testifies to the serious and earnest nature of Simon's mind, to his thirst for knowledge and to his deeply religious disposition, while it matured those broad and popular sympathies that were later to so endear him to the people.

The beautiful legends that told of happenings at the death of bishop Grosseteste, and the miracles said to have been performed at his shrine, show that he was revered as a saint. On the night of his death bells were heard in the sky by the bishop of London; some friars, on their way to Bugden, where he died, heard heavenly music in the air, the music made by angels come down to earth to take his soul. Years later, on the Sunday before the battle of Evesham, a lad was brought to the bishop's tomb to be healed of dumbness and contortions. He fell asleep and slept long; on waking he began to speak and told his parents it was needless to wait longer, for the bishop was not present; he was gone to Evesham to help Earl Simon, his brother, who was to die there.

By the end of the year 1251 Simon de Montfort was again in England and enough in favour with the king to be taken to York for the Christmas festivities and the marriage of King Henry's daughter Margaret, then in her tenth year, to the young king of Scotland, Alexander III, who was about twelve.

Back in Gascony again after these festivities Simon continued his stern rule there. The castled brigands had acquired such strength during his absence that he found himself sorely pressed by them in a manner that called forth all his energies as a soldier. It was with the utmost difficulty that he was able to preserve the mastery over them in one battle, during which he was himself unhorsed and his life in danger; at another time he was blockaded by them in an unprovisioned town from which, however, he extracted himself by personal bravery. It was said that the Gascons feared him "as a thunderbolt". It is indeed probable, from what we know of the fiery temper of Simon de Montfort, that he quenched rebellion sharply and sternly. He was not the man to bear gently with the open and secret resistance that he met. But it is not likely that much would have been heard of the complaints against him had not the king's ever-suspicious ear drunk in only too greedily all that the enemies of his great lieutenant chose to pour into it. The voices of the lower orders and the merchants whom Simon had protected by destroying the robbers' nests unfortunately could not be heard, nor did news reach the king of the way in which peace had been made between Simon and many citizens. Whether recognized by the king or not, however, his work showed the beginnings of those constitutional principles and that sympathy with the common people that was to characterize his later life.

But the clamour of his enemies travelled across the sea and found easy entrance at the English court. Accordingly, a committee of eleven English nobles was set up by the king in January 1252 to examine the justice of Simon's appeals to the king for aid and the complaints of the Gascon rebels.

Simon, finding himself accused behind his back of extortion and tyranny, hastened to England to meet his accusers face to face. A most extraordinary scene

followed; like many weak people, King Henry lost his temper easily and he screamed threats, reproaches and insults at his lieutenant in Gascony, even implying that Simon was a traitor. At this, the ultimate insult to a medieval knight, the affronted earl lost all command of his impetuous temper and in direct terms openly told the king that were he not protected by the kingly authority "like an umbrella" this would be an evil hour for him.

"Who can believe you to be a Christian or that you go to confession, for of what use would that be without repentance and atonement?" cried the earl in a bitter rage. The king, though goaded by these retorts, did not dare to order his arrest.

"Never did I repent of aught so much as allowing you to enter England," he replied, "and win honour and land therein which now so puff you up!"

The quarrel reached such violence that their friends were obliged to step in and break up the dispute.

It is interesting to note here how different was the attitude of the English barons towards Simon. Sixteen years before they had joined together to try to thrust him from the country as an alien and an upstart, and it was all the king could do to protect him from their wrath. Now they joined together to protect him from the injustice of the king.

King Henry then decided to hand over Gascony to his son Edward, now in his thirteenth year, and a settlement was eventually reached whereby Simon gave up all the remainder of his term of office in Gascony in return for the sum of 7,000 marks. He then withdrew from turbulent Gascony into France, where he was offered many honours, including the office of high steward. This he declined, saying that he was "unwilling to prove a renegade" from the service of the king who had called him a traitor but a few months before.

XVII

The Mad Parliament

WE DO not know much of Simon de Montfort's movements during the fateful years that led up to the tremendously important revolution of 1258 when the barons decided to take matters into their own hands, to control their king and to reform the lawless state of the land. He acted as envoy or ambassador for King Henry in France and Scotland from time to time; we get the impression that at times the king tried to conciliate him and at others tried to keep him well out of the way.

Meanwhile conditions in England had not improved and many murmurings of discontent were heard throughout the land. The wet summer of 1257 had resulted in a very bad harvest and it was followed by a hard winter and a late cold spring. A terrible famine was the result and in the early part of the year 1258 so many people died of hunger that their bodies were left lying on the roadside. Horseflesh and even the bark of trees became articles of food. The king seized fifty vessels laden with corn which his brother, Richard of Cornwall, sent in to London from abroad, but the Londoners resisted this breach of their charter with such effect that the king was forced to come into the market like others, with the only advantage of buying his corn there at 2d a quarter below the market price. To add to the general misery of the country the Welsh were once more attacking and harrying the border.

In April 1258 King Henry called his barons to the parliament of which we have already read in Chapter 6. Here he planned to persuade them to grant him more money for his own debts, to meet new tax demands from the pope and for the reckless and ill-advised Sicilian enterprise upon which he wished to embark.

Simon de Montfort and several of the barons however, decided that the time had come to make a determined stand against the king. An eye-witness account says, "On the day agreed upon, as the third hour approached, the earls, barons and knights came to Westminster in great array, in their complete suits of mail, with their swords by their sides. At the entrance of the royal chamber they laid down their weapons, and when they appeared before the king, saluted him with the reverence that was due to him."

In spite of this the king was seized with a sudden terror at their threatening aspect and asked them if he was their prisoner. The barons told him of the reforms they wanted, and so firm and united a front did they show that he gave way and swore on the relics of St Edward to do as they wished and to call another parliament at Oxford in June of that year. The chronicler of the times was especially struck with the determined attitude of Simon de Montfort on this occasion and wrote: "As of old Simon Maccabaeus had risen in arms for his father Judah, so Simon de Montfort rose to defend the liberties and rights of England." It is now that Simon emerges for the first time as leader and spokesman for the barons.

The king felt extremely resentful and humiliated at this attempt to curb his powers and held his brother-in-law Simon chiefly responsible for this. His resentment shows clearly in this story related by Matthew Paris.

One day, in the extreme heat of that summer, the king had left Westminster and embarked on the Thames to have dinner out of doors. Suddenly the sky became overcast, thunder growled and torrents of rain fell amid flashes of lightning. The king, alarmed by the violence of the storm, ordered his servants to put in to shore. The boat was discovered to be in front of the bishop of Durham's palace, where Simon de Montfort was lodging at the time. Simon at once appeared with smiling face and, saluting the king respectfully, asked, "What are you afraid of? The storm has already passed."

The king answered in a mortified tone, "I am extremely afraid of the thunder and the flashes, but by God's head I am more afraid of you than of all the thunder and lightning in the whole world."

"Sir," replied the earl, "it is not myself, your constant friend, the faithful servant of king and country, that you should fear, but your enemies and deceivers who live on falsehood and pillage."

That famous assembly, which was to earn the title of

the Mad Parliament, met at Oxford on the appointed day, 11 June, 1258.

The sunlight flickered on lances and flashed on steel and mail as the great feudal array of barons and lesser lords and their retainers rode fully armed into Oxford. Students and scholars, clerks and friars all crowded the streets shouting for reform and change. The sullen anger of the people against blatant misrule had changed to a flame of hope and resolve.

All around the hall where the parliament was held were ranks of horsemen, and the rows of banners, a bright mass of colour in the sunshine, glittered with the blazons of the greatest names in England. The king hated the thought of the new reforms, but his barons had encircled him with an iron ring of steel. During the stormy sessions of debate they left their swords outside the door but in their grim determination the king was only too well aware of the power of these swords. Prince Edward, or the Lord Edward as he was often called, heir to the realm and now an ardent noble youth of twenty-one, was even more bitter than his father at the curbing of the royal power; but he, like the king, would in the end take the oath to uphold the Provisions of Oxford, as the new reforms were called, for they could not stand against the collected force and the iron will of the barons.

Debating for nearly a month, the barons finally won through with their plans to reform the kingdom. Simon de Montfort himself, if we are to believe a witness, is said to have shown some repugnance against the Provisions, seeing their impracticability and realizing the difficulties that would arise from them. It was only after much discussion that he agreed to swear to them, saying: "By the arm of St James, though I take this oath last of all and against my will, yet will I keep it inviolate, and none shall hinder me." He took the oath as a solemn religious tie upon his conscience and was never to break it, in spite of what his colleagues were later to do. As an immediate earnest of his good faith, being a foreigner himself, he gave up his castles of Kenilworth and Odiham, and called upon the other foreigners to follow suit.

Supporting the king were first and foremost his own relations, his half-brothers and the earl of Warenne, and also John Mansel, provost of Beverley. He had served the crown for sixteen years at least, and had risen to great wealth but little honour in its service. These men had drawn the hatred of the kingdom upon themselves and were unworthy advisers to the king.

Opposing the king were Simon de Montfort, Walter de Cantilupe, bishop of Worcester, the earls of Gloucester, Norfolk and Hereford, John Balliol (founder of Balliol college, Oxford), Hugh le Despenser and many others.

Some of these held firm to their ideals to the end, but some later went over to the king's side.

The Prince Edward, taller than most men, rash, bold and quick to wrath, made no attempt to veil his rage as he took the oath. His natural ability at fighting had already been well proved. Since the prince's marriage in 1254, King Henry had put him in possession of the earldom of Chester and also of Ireland, Gascony, the Channel Islands and the king's lands in Wales – in short, of all the most troublesome parts of the realm. As earl of Chester he had had plenty of opportunities of winning his spurs in fighting with Llywelyn, prince of Wales. Keeping order among the border lords in Wales had kept him away from court and he was in no way involved with his father's errors and misrule. For this reason the barons had some hopes of persuading him over to their side.

On the day that the king finally agreed to swear to the new laws the barons left behind their ringed mail and their helmets and swords and rode to the hall in silks and velvets, attended only by their squires and pages instead of armed men. They wished to quieten the fears of the king and to allay the wrath of the young prince by showing that their rule would be lawful, that they were true and loyal subjects acting only for the good of the kingdom.

The king's half-brothers, and many alien officials hurling defiance at the barons, refused to give up their castles or to take the oath. When told that they must either swear the oath or go into exile, they left the hall and rode away.

When it became known that the Provisions were signed all the bells in Oxford rang out and the people waiting in the streets surged through the town singing and shouting. There was great rejoicing and great hopes of better times throughout the land.

XVIII

Civil War Draws Near

IT WAS soon discovered that the king's half-brothers and other foreigners had fled from Oxford to Winchester. The barons broke up the parliament and, taking the king with them, they marched on Winchester. Here the fugitives were besieged and soon reduced to submission. They then agreed to swear to the Provisions of Oxford but the barons insisted on their exile. Before they went, they attended a great banquet in the bishop's palace, where some of the principal guests, including the earl of Gloucester and the abbot of Westminster, were taken ill with symptoms of poisoning. The earl's brother William indeed died, but the earl himself, thanks to the care of his physician, a Dominican monk, escaped after a tedious illness with the loss of his hair, his nails and teeth nearly dropping out and his skin peeling away. The sudden illness and death of so many persons of note naturally gave rise to suspicions of foul play, but the evidence of poison against the departing aliens (though in the temper of the times readily believed) appears very slight. Concealed stores of poison were said to be found, yet the same illness attacked others after the exiles had gone and suspicions were then transferred to the cooks.

Young Henry de Montfort, eldest son of Earl Simon, with fresh memories of their insults to his father, followed the exiles to France and prevailed upon the French king to show them no favour beyond that of a safe passage to Poitou. Their final departure from England removed one great obstacle to reform and gave King Henry a new chance of regaining his popularity with his subjects.

From Winchester the council of barons went on to London, anxious to make certain of the support of the city for the new laws. Owing to the dangerous illness of the earl of Gloucester the publication of the Oxford Provisions was deferred until 18 October 1258, when they were solemnly proclaimed, together with Magna Carta, in every county in Latin, French and English. This was the first time that English as well as French was used in an official document since the days of William the Conqueror and shows the anxiety of the barons to explain their conduct to the people at large.

Dover and other castles were put into English hands; Simon handed back to the king his castles of Kenilworth and Odiham but he had received Winchester from the king instead. The baronial council now ruled England and matters proceeded smoothly, if uneasily, for a time, but a feeling of discontent and confusion was abroad in the land and hostility towards the new regime began to grow. Nature, too, increased the trouble. An unusually fine harvest was almost entirely destroyed by heavy rain and floods and, like a great undertone of misery, the shortage of food continued throughout the country. Matters were probably not worse than they had been before 1258, but the fact that they were not better was enough to cause discontent with the barons' party, which had entered into power with such high hopes and promises. Complaints were brought to Prince Edward that whereas the king had accepted the Provisions laid down at Oxford the barons themselves had "done nothing of what they had promised for the good of the realm". Simon de Montfort, angry that the barons were not keeping their solemn oath, left England for France, saying that he perferred to die without a foot of land rather than live in perjury and falsehood.

The king himself was also much in France during this time. The Oxford Provisions were naturally hateful to him and he considered that as the barons were not keeping their share of the pact he was therefore not bound to keep his, and he began to press the pope to give him a bull absolving him from his oath to observe them. In spite of letters from the barons explaining their reforms the pope was not best pleased at the turn of events in England and King Henry had high hopes of obtaining what he wanted.

In the spring of 1263 the baronial party appealed to Simon de Montfort to come back to England and lead it. Simon had been busy in France with peace treaties and had not as yet been in complete opposition to the king; but their frequent quarrels and the growing proof of King Henry's disregard for the sanctity of his oath finally decided Simon to throw himself into definite and active opposition and to refuse to allow the king to go back on his sworn word. He returned to England and the barons' party rallied round him.

Many changes had transformed this party from the original group that had drawn up the provisions of Oxford. Death and defection had wrought havoc in its ranks. The earl of Norfolk and his brother had gone over to the king's side. The immensely rich and powerful earl of Gloucester had died. The young "Red Gilbert", his heir, was typical of the new character of the barons' party. As well as Simon and his devoted followers it was composed of vigorous young enthusiasts more anxious for their own rights than anything else. They wanted Simon de Montfort for their leader because of his great ability and prestige, but they did not share his stern, uncompromising high-minded principles and were soon to fall away when matters went against them.

Now for a time Prince Edward came under the influence of his uncle Simon de Montfort and it almost seemed that he might join the barons' party. The innate nobility of character and warm impulses of the young prince, his sense of honour and justice and that sympathy for the oppressed which he had already shown, were enough to encourage such hopes, and it was at about this time that he knighted Simon's two elder sons.

This news angered the king and many rumours began to spread that he was collecting an army of foreign mercenaries in France to help him resume absolute rule. Before many months had passed, to the shocked dismay of all who had hoped for peace and justice, he arrived back in England with 300 foreign paid knights and a papal bull absolving him from his oath to uphold the Provisions of Oxford. Now began a time of great tension likely to explode into civil war. The king hastened at once to the strongest of all his fortresses, the Tower of London, and from there attempted to crush his enemies. He committed all his crown jewels to the custody of his sister-in-law, the queen of France, as a security to raise money, a practice not unusual in that age. In the list, besides his great crown, three golden crowns, and five "garlands" or circlets for the head, were another three golden crowns, fifty-two clasps, sixty-two girdles, two hundred and eight jewelled rings, and two golden peacocks that poured sweet waters from their beaks.

Simon de Montfort and his party, with Prince Edward, remained outside the London city walls. Prince Edward tried to see his father, but the king, angered by his son's friendship with Simon, refused to admit him.

"Let not my son Edward appear before me, because if I see him, I will not keep myself from kissing him," he said, afraid that his wish to be firm with his rebellious son would not stand the strain of a personal meeting.

King Henry's brother, Richard of Cornwall, was called in to make peace between father and son and after a week of steady persuasion he was successful, for soon after this Prince Edward broke with his uncle Simon completely and returned to the royal side.

Several things had happened to change the prince's

views. The new young earl of Gloucester, Simon's ally, had refused to do homage to him as heir to the throne; Simon had agreed to give his daughter in marriage to Prince Edward's old enemy, Prince Llywelyn of Wales; and finally the Londoners had gravely insulted his mother the queen. She had become more unpopular than ever by reason of her extravagance and mismanagement of the king's affairs when he was abroad. A London mob, led by one of the powerful barons, had raised a dreadful uproar against the unhappy Jews, whose wealth had excited their envy. They killed and plundered many of these wretched people without mercy and the queen in the Tower was seized with mortal terror at the outrageous yells of the mob. She got into her barge on the river with many of her great ladies, intending to escape by water to Windsor. But the raging people, to whom she had rendered herself most hateful, made a general rush to the bridge as soon as they saw the royal barge on the river, crying "Drown the witch! Drown the witch!" At the same time they pelted the queen and her ladies with mud, yelling insults at them and trying to sink the barge by hurling down upon it blocks of wood and stone of an enormous weight, which they tore from the unfinished buildings of the bridge. The poor ladies were also pelted with rotten eggs and sheeps' bones and everything vile. Terrified of the barge being swamped or dashed to pieces the queen and her ladies with difficulty escaped the fury of the mob by returning to the Tower.

The high-spirited Prince Edward, who adored his mother, never forgave the Londoners for this insult, and never again did he stray from the royal side.

XIX

Flames of Battle over England

THE WHOLE country was now trembling on the brink of civil war. As a last resort both sides agreed to seek the arbitration of King Louis IX of France. Saint Louis, as he was known, was famous for his judicial decisions; his uprightness was unquestioned and he was respected by all, so the whole question of the Provisions of Oxford was laid before him. He was a firm believer in royal authority and his decision, given in what was called the Mise of Amiens, was that, while Magna Carta was binding on the king of England and that he had no right to disregard it, the position in which King Henry had been placed by the Mad Parliament was quite illegal and that the Provisions of Oxford were void. No subjects, King Louis declared, had the right to deprive their sovereign of the custody of his castles, nor of the choice of his ministers.

This meant that Simon de Montfort and his supporters had to choose between breaking their oath to uphold the Provisions or fighting for them. They chose to fight, and the smouldering embers were fanned into the flames of civil war – the Barons' War.

King Henry hastened to place his adored queen in safety in France and, having taken a tender leave of her, returned to join Prince Edward at Windsor. The prince, having returned from a victorious campaign in

King Louis IX of France.

Wales and finding himself without money to pay his troops (which he knew his father's cause would soon need) marched straightway to the Temple in London. Here he told the master that it was his pleasure to see the jewels of the queen his mother, as he understood they were not safely kept. On this excuse he and his men entered the treasury and broke open with sledge hammers the coffers of many persons who had lodged their money there in the hands of the Templars and seized £10,000 belonging to the citizens of London. This, together with the queen's jewels, they carried off to the royal fortress of Windsor.

London seethed with violence and many foreigners there fled to Windsor to join the royal party, while others left it by fleeing abroad. The king's favourite adviser, John Mansel, known as the richest clerk in England, was one of those who secretly fled abroad, taking with him some of the foreign ladies.

Simon de Montfort, now supreme head of the barons' party, took the law into his own hands. The noble youth of England streamed towards his cause in great numbers. Almost everywhere the middle classes were on his side and he had the hearty support of the friars. Young Henry of Almain, eldest son of Richard of Cornwall, had returned from abroad and was a new and enthusiastic convert to the barons' cause.

Simon led his forces first of all westwards, to the border country where the earl of Gloucester's strength lay and where the Welsh might form a support in case of need. Through the long June days of 1263 they marched from one royal stronghold to another. They attacked the hated foreign bishop of Hereford in his own church and shut him up in the castle of Eardisley, taking all his goods and dividing them up among themselves. Much needless violence was done, though Simon issued orders that no sacred building was to be touched, under penalty of death. This did little to stop the wholesale destruction. The wildness of his followers was to bring much trouble to Simon, and even his friends could see that the lawlessness of these doings would drive away the friends of law and order. In the affair of the bishop of Hereford, Simon's son, the young Henry de Montfort, had distinguished himself, showing already that rashness which was to be such an obstacle to his father's success.

From the border countries Simon led his forces eastwards. Richard of Cornwall, always eager to mediate, tried to meet him at Wallingford, but the earl refused to see him and pressed on towards Dover, for it was essential for him to secure the sea ports. He moved with great rapidity. On 29 June he reached Reading, the day after he arrived at Guildford; the next day he was at Reigate, and soon after he reached Dover. From Dover he marched with his victorious army to London. He entered the town at once and was received with all signs of joy by the citizens.

A kind of truce now seems to have taken place and Simon retired to his own stronghold of Kenilworth to await events. During this interval he was to suffer another turn of fortune's wheel, for many of his supporters began to desert his cause. The first to go was young Henry of Almain, who told him that he could not fight against his father and his uncle the king, but neither would he draw his sword against the earl; whereupon Simon told him that it was not his sword that he dreaded but his fickle nature and told him to go and do as he pleased, for he feared him not. "But I and my four sons," he continued, "though all should desert me, will stand fast for the cause I have sworn to defend, for the honour of the church and the welfare of the realm."

In spite of these words the desertion of Henry of Almain hurt Simon deeply, and seeds of hatred were sown between Simon's sons and their cousin, which were later to bring them all to a violent and bloody end.

The earl of Warenne and other important barons also left Simon and went over to the royalist side, encouraged by Prince Edward, who had taken control and was remaking the royal party. Simon's support was indeed weakened and well might he exclaim, "I have been in many lands and among many nations, pagan and Christian, but in no race have I ever found such faithlessness and deceit as I have met in England." Was it perhaps Simon's stern and rigid uncompromising nature that alienated these supporters? From what we can learn of him from those monks who wrote their eye-witness chronicles of those days his was not the nature to unbend or deviate from his unswerving course to suit his followers.

The truce did not last long and King Henry was the first to break it. He and Prince Edward, with many of the leading nobles, suddenly marched on Dover. Possession of its castle was essential to the royal cause, for it was the gateway into England.

Simon's supporters in Dover castle held firm and refused to admit the royalists, who, disappointed, turned to London, hoping by a rapid march to surprise the town. Simon moved quickly from Kenilworth to its rescue. A clever trap was laid for him, which almost proved successful.

He was lying in Southwark when the king's forces came up and, not being strong enough to meet them, he tried to escape into the city. Four rich London citizens sent word to the king that they could take the earl prisoner. They locked the city gates against him and threw the keys into the river. But as the royalist army came thundering up the citizens broke down the gates with battering rams and opened them to the earl and his men. The four traitors would have been torn limb from limb by the mob, but the earl saved them from this vengeance and sent them as prisoners to Kenilworth.

Shortly after this incident Simon's horse fell with him and he broke his leg. Carried by litter back to Kenilworth he was obliged to wait there with what patience he could muster until it mended. Meanwhile he sent his sons to the border country again. They besieged and took Radnor castle and entered Gloucester by trickery. Two of their knights disguised themselves as wool merchants and persuaded the gatekeepers to open the gates and let them in to trade. Once inside they threw off their wool-merchants cloaks and showed themselves fully armed. The frightened gatekeepers threw them the keys and the barons' army streamed in to take possession of the city.

Prince Edward, in hot pursuit, attacked them there, but failed to force his way into the town. He nevertheless made his way into the castle by means of a boat across the moat and repelled all the attacks of the barons, until the arrival of the earl of Derby with reinforcements for the barons forced him to parley. In the presence of the bishop of Worcester, Prince Edward discussed terms with his cousin Henry de Montfort; and Henry de Montfort believed the prince's word that he would observe a truce and that he would have his father the king bow to the will of the barons in all things. Blind to the danger of the prince's trickery Henry de Montfort called off the barons' army and took it back to Kenilworth. No sooner had they gone than Prince Edward broke his word and the truce. He seized many of the citizens and punished them with fines and imprisonment, after which he hurried off to join the king.

Earl Simon was greatly annoyed at this disaster, and with good cause, for had he captured Prince Edward – as he might well have done by blockade – he would have had the king at his mercy. The incompetence shown by Simon's sons, in military no less than in other matters, is remarkable and was finally to cost their father his life.

XX

The Battle of Lewes

IN THE early spring of 1264 the royalist armies rallied at Oxford and Prince Edward came there to join his father. The university students, all in favour of the Oxford Provisions, had given vent to their feelings in a fierce quarrel with the townspeople just before the king's arrival. The king therefore dismissed the university because of the danger to the students of rough treatment from his soldiery. The students marched out in a body, 15,000 strong it is said, and joined the barons' army.

Simon de Montfort meanwhile had recovered sufficiently from his broken leg to become mobile again and was moving towards London, having left his son Simon with a strong force to hold Northampton. On Passion Sunday, the 5 April, the king and Prince Edward attacked and captured this town. They gained entrance because the French monks of the priory of St Andrew's, anxious to help them, had undermined the walls, putting in wooden props as a temporary support, so that a breach was easily made. The barons made a gallant resistance, but their leader, the young Simon de Montfort, was taken prisoner and the rest surrendered, to the number of fifteen barons and sixty knights. A brave band of Oxford students, who had fought with slings, bows and crossbows under their own banner, were also taken prisoner.

On hearing of this Earl Simon was much moved by the loss of his son and "raging like a lion robbed of his whelps" vowed that before the end of May the fortunes of war should be reversed. He then decided to take Rochester, a royalist castle near London.

On Good Friday, 18 April, he forced an entrance to the city by sending a fireboat, all alight with blazing pitch, sulphur coals and pork fat, to burn down a fortified bridge. In the evening the barons' army broke in and plundered the city, stealing the gold and silver from the church of St Andrew and stabling their horses in it. Both sides stopped fighting on Easter Sunday but started again on Easter Monday. The royalist garrison held out in the massive Norman keep of the castle and Simon, hearing that the king was threatening London from the north, withdrew his forces.

The king however merely raised the siege of Rochester castle and hastened on to Kent and the coast, where he may have hoped to find ships to sail up the Thames to London. He found however that on Earl Simon's orders every ship had put to sea. The king hoped to occupy the channel ports for he knew that his queen in France was busy collecting an army of mercenaries to come over and help him. But Earl Simon and his small army still held London and Dover castle and now, reinforced by a levy of Londoners, they marched for the coast, pursuing the great royalist force, and determined to bring it to battle.

The king's army left the coast and made for Lewes town. As they moved through the tracks and pathways of the Sussex Weald they were constantly harried by the green-clad bowmen of the Weald who, fighting for Earl Simon, picked them off with their arrows from the shelter of the woods and copses.

Earl Simon and his army were guided through the forests of the Weald by more bowmen and they encamped at Fletching village, near Lewes. The earl travelled in a carriage, for his leg was not yet entirely mended. As they camped for the night among the thickets of the green forest outside the village news was brought to them that the king had reached Lewes and was lodged in the Cluniac priory, and that Prince Edward was in the castle.

Simon determined on one last bid for peace and at dawn next day he sent the bishops of London and Worcester with a letter to the king offering peace with every concession in keeping with honour. With an escort of lords, knights, friars and clerks, they rode with the scroll down through the wooded valley of the river Ouse to Lewes, while the encamped barons' army watched and waited.

When the bishops and their escort returned all could see from their faces that the peace mission had failed. They told how they had scarcely stated their terms before the king and the great lords about him broke into a clamour of scorn and fury. The king's reply, which the bishops now handed to Earl Simon, was full of wrath and defiance. A second letter from Richard of Cornwall and Prince Edward denounced Simon de Montfort, Gilbert de Clare, earl of Gloucester, and all their accomplices as traitors and challenged them to do their worst. Richard of Cornwall had put off his old character of mediator, for the destruction of his property in London by the barons' army had infuriated him. While passing through London they had burned down his manor and ruined his carefully built fishpond, letting out both the water and the fish. As for Prince Edward, he was not likely either to forgive or forget the insults put upon his mother by the Londoners and he burned for revenge. After these answers Earl Simon resolved to waste no more time and next day, Wednesday, 14 May 1265, the fate of the country was decided on the battlefield of Lewes.

As evening closed in upon his waiting army Earl Simon bestowed the accolade of knighthood upon the young earls of Gloucester and Oxford and others of his young followers. To be thus knighted on the field was a great honour and the ardent young supporters of the earl were filled with his own enthusiasm and burned with the sense of the justice of their cause as they buckled on their swords and armour and prepared for battle. They all wore over their armour surcoats with white crosses on the back and front to distinguish them, for in full mail armour all men were apt to look alike.

Long before dawn next day the army moved off in a long file through the darkness, led by Earl Simon astride his great black war horse. His banner, the fork-tailed Blanche Lion of Montfort, was carried by his standard bearer, Sir William le Blound. Guided by Sussex men of the Weald, they reached Offham, and there turned off the road and went up a steep track to the heights of Offham Hill. Here they found a solitary sentry of the royalist army fast asleep in the shelter of a gorse bush.

Prodded awake by the earl's men he doubtless gave them valuable information.

Now the whole army, some 5,000 strong, had gained the ridge overlooking the town of Lewes. Earl Simon galloped up and down arranging his army in its battle order. In the forefront were the thin lines of knights armed with their lances, swords, battle-axes and maces, while the green-clad archers and slingers were in the rear. The left wing was formed of the London levies commanded by Sir Henry de Hastings and Sir Nicholas de Segrave, and the centre by the young earl of Gloucester, eager to show himself worthy of his newly gained spurs. The right wing was commanded by Earl Simon's two sons, Henry and Guy. The earl himself took command of a fourth force which he kept in reserve at the rear, ready to hurl itself into the fray wherever it was needed.

Simon knew that much of the royalist army thought that he was still unable to be on horseback because of the accident to his leg and he placed the carriage in which he had travelled in a prominent position at the top of the hill with his standard planted beside it. Inside it were imprisoned the four London traitors who had barred the gates of the city against him and he hoped that the royalists would be misled into attacking it.

When all was ready and the whole army poised in its battle array the earl wheeled his great charger round and, raising his sword, called upon his followers to pray for victory in the justice of their cause and to commend their souls to God. The whole army dismounted and each man dropped down full length upon the ground, spreading out his arms as if to form a cross, and prayed aloud to God for victory on that day.

As the sun slowly rose and began to gleam on the bell-tower of the priory, down below in Lewes town some grooms, who had come out to graze the horses of the royalist army, looked up in astonishment and saw the whole of earl Simon's army poised in menace along the top of the hill. They fled back in terror to raise the alarm.

Within moments the royal trumpets were sounding through the town and royalist soldiers were rushing through the streets, buckling on their armour as they ran. Quickly afield and straight in the saddle Prince Edward came galloping out of the castle with his lords, his leopard banners streaming behind him. The royalist army, some 9,000 strong, had little time to marshal in battle array with Prince Edward on the right in front of the castle, Richard of Cornwall on the left with the Scottish lords and King Henry, with his great dragon standard "of red samite embroidered with gold, the tongue appearing as if continually moving, and the eyes of sapphire" in the centre.

Hardly were they thus massed when, with trumpets sounding and swords raised high, Earl Simon's knights charged down upon them. The royalist forces charged forward and both sides met with a splintering clash. There were savage struggles as the knights battled furiously, often against their own kinsmen on the opposing side, while Simon's archers from behind and higher up the hill sent their arrows winging into the steel lines of struggling men.

"Oh, wretched sight," laments the chronicler William

of Rishanger, "when the son strives to overpower the father and the father the son; kinsman against kinsman, fellow citizen against fellow citizen, with their swords brandished on either side, drunk with the gore of the slain, felling, maiming, and trampling their foes under the horses feet, or binding their prisoners alive in the straitest bonds."

Prince Edward meanwhile had charged with his force in a headlong attack upon the Londoners of Simon's left wing. These, being lightly armed and ill-trained, offered little resistance to his charge. They scattered and fled, but the prince who, as the chronicler recorded "thirsted after their blood as the hart pants for cooling stream" pursued them relentlessly and cut them down as they fled. Sixty of them drowned in the river Ouse and Prince Edward's nobles cut down some of them as far away as Croydon.

When he had sufficiently glutted his sword with the blood of the Londoners and bitterly avenged the insult they had put upon his mother, the prince and his men were turning back towards the battlefield when they saw the carriage on the hill with Earl Simon's standard flying beside it. Thinking the earl was within they made a savage attack upon it, crying, "Come out, Simon, thou devil!" Sir William de Blound was killed defending the standard and the four wretched traitors within the carriage were put to the sword before they could prove their identity to their friends.

By the time Prince Edward returned to the main battlefield he found that Earl Simon had won the battle, for, as soon as he saw the best troops of the enemy engaged in pursuing the least valuable part of his own force, the earl had hurled the rest of his army upon that body of royalists which was led by King Henry and his brother in person, and, after a fierce struggle, had routed them at all points.

The king, who had fought bravely and had two horses killed under him, was driven back into the priory and the battle continued round its walls for some time. Richard of Cornwall, who fought his way uphill, was surrounded and forced to take refuge in a windmill. Here he was taunted with shouts of "Come down! thou bad miller!" The windmill being no place to withstand a long siege he came down and surrendered to Sir John Gifford, one of the earl of Gloucester's knights.

Many of the vanquished were left dead upon the field and many were driven into the marshes and brown mud near the river Ouse where they stuck fast in the slime and were drowned. Next day with the ebbing tide many were found still astride their horses, upright in their saddles with their arms stretched out and their swords still in their hands, as though they were still alive.

Thus Prince Edward came back to find his uncle a prisoner, his father surrounded without a chance to escape and the greater part of the royalist forces routed or slain. He burned to renew the battle but many of his followers, seeing that all was lost, took to flight. The prince, thus deserted, took sanctuary with the few that were left to him in the priory.

The priory, the last stronghold of the royalists, would probably have been quickly taken by storm had not wiser counsels prevailed and the fall of darkness put an end to the conflict.

At nightfall a truce was made. Prince Edward surrendered himself as hostage for his father and Prince Henry of Almain did the same for his father. The victory of Simon de Montfort and the barons' army was complete.

XXI

Victorious Simon now Rules England

THE KING was not long in suing for peace and he signed a treaty with Simon de Montfort which is known to history as the Mise of Lewes.

The number of dead after the battle of Lewes has been estimated at 2,700, yet very few of the leaders were killed. The royalist forces lost only two nobles and the baronial forces also lost two. Nobles were of far greater value as prisoners for ransom than as corpses, and the excellent quality of plate helmets and mail armour at that time probably also accounts for so little bloodshed among the nobility. It is interesting to hear that in the year 1810 three burial pits near the modern prison of Lewes were opened and 1,500 skeletons were discovered.

From Lewes Earl Simon, having deposited his less noble prisoners in safe places, but taking the king with him, moved to London, where he summoned a parliament to meet in June, 1264. Here for the first time four knights from each county were summoned to attend. Here the magnates, prelates and others present entrusted the establishment of a provisional administration to Simon de Montfort, the earl of Gloucester and the bishop of Chichester. A council of nine, chosen by these three, was to advise the king, and three of these were always to be in attendance upon him. These three were always to supervise affairs of state and to advise the king on changes in the council of nine and to settle matters in dispute between them. Simon de Montfort remained the power behind the throne while the royal household, the chancery and the exchequer continued to function in the king's name under the supervision of the council of nine. Simon's faithful adherence to the Provisions of Oxford required him to insist on this. In his own eyes he was still the faithful vassal entrusted to maintain the co-operation, through a council, of king and community.

In reality however, Simon de Montfort reigned supreme. "All things were ordered by him," we are told; "the king had but the shadow of royalty." The church and the people remained faithful to their champion. This is plainly shown by the remarkable poem *The Song of Lewes*, which was written at this time. It begins with an elaborate defence of Simon's policy, both before and after the battle of Lewes, and tells of the joy of all England at the release from so many evils. It proceeds to defend Simon from the charge of deceit and cunning. "Far from it," exclaims the writer, "he has ever been true and constant, and has maintained the good cause in the teeth of death; he alone has kept the oath he swore. He would not have acted as he has acted," continues the poem, "had he looked to his own advantage; he has sacrified himself for the good of others. His is not the cunning which intrigues for a secret object, he fights in the sight of heaven and gives himself, like his master Christ, unto death for the many. His cause must be favoured of God or he would not have won the victory over such foes." With Simon's "faith and fidelity" is compared the treachery that Prince Edward showed at Gloucester and elsewhere. "The Prince is like the leopard, beautiful but faithless. Had he and his won the day, England would have been lost for ever; but praise be to God who had given the earl the victory, for his enemies are the enemies of heaven, the church and the country."

Such was the enthusiasm that Simon excited in men

like the writer of this remarkable song of triumph; and the same strain of praise is kept up in other songs of the time. His name of Montfort is referred to as "the strong mount" to which his friends look for protection and the feeling towards him is nothing less than veneration.

But in spite of Simon's popularity at home, there was great danger of invasion from abroad, for the queen had, during that summer, assembled a large army on the coast of Flanders. This army was commanded by those royalists who had escaped from Lewes and waited only for a favourable breeze to cross over to England. Earl Simon made strenuous efforts to meet this danger and called upon every county in England to defend the coasts. The people felt the common danger and flocked to defend their country. The wind continued unfavourable, the people held firm, and the foreign troops waited in vain until, with the approach of winter, they melted away, and the danger passed. Peace returned for a brief spell to the harassed land.

In spite of the support of the greater part of the commoners and the church, Simon's position with the greater barons was daily becoming more difficult and unsatisfactory. Quarrels over the ransoms of prisoners and the unruly behaviour of Simon's four sons did nothing to improve this. His eldest son Henry was nicknamed the "wool merchant" because he seized for his own use the wool that was brought into the ports. The younger sons plundered vessels in the Channel and naturally all this was bitterly resented by the barons. Of all his party his own sons seem to have done him as much mischief as any; but he loved them only too well and probably overlooked acts of violence and impudence on their part which it would have been wiser to check with a strong hand.

Prince Edward was lodged as a prisoner in Wallingford castle and one of his favourite knights, Sir Warren de Basingbourne, made a desperate attempt to rescue him. Crossing the country with 300 horsemen he arrived at

Wallingford just as the sun rose, made a fierce attack on the castle and won the outermost wall. The besieged defended themselves furiously with crossbows and battle engines; at last they called out to Sir Warren that if they wanted Prince Edward they should have him, but bound hand and foot and shot from the mangonel (a vast machine used for casting huge stones). As soon as the prince heard of this cruel intention he demanded leave to speak with his friends and, coming out onto the wall, he told them that if they persevered he would be destroyed. Whereupon Sir Warren and his chevaliers retired in great dejection.

After this Earl Simon transferred his royal prisoner to Kenilworth castle for safe keeping. His aunt the countess was residing there and she offered him all the solace she could.

XXII

Simon Calls the Famous Parliament of 1265

SIMON celebrated the Christmas of 1264 with great pomp and festivity at Kenilworth, his vast household being further swelled by 140 knights and numerous supporters. But behind all the lavish display his gnawing worries lurked.

The peace that he had won by force had still to be turned into a real peace; the national rally of the previous summer had to be given a political character. Before he had returned home to Kenilworth for Christmas he had made the king send out summons for a great parliament to be held in London on 20 January, 1265. The settlement which he hoped to reach once and for all would necessarily comprise judicial proceedings at this great meeting. Matters had not gone as he had hoped since the battle of Lewes and a new start had to be made.

It is significant that only five earls and eighteen barons, all strong supporters of Simon, were summoned to this parliament, and shows his increased reliance on the middle classes, for many barons had returned to the king's side. Writs to others, for example John Balliol and the northern royalists, were sent out later in an effort to get their support. All the bishops – Simon of Norwich later than the others – and more than a hundred heads of religious houses were summoned, as well as two knights from each shire, and, for the first time in the history of England, "two of the more discreet, lawful and trustworthy of their citizens or burgesses" from York, Lincoln and other boroughs of the realm. Four men from Sandwich and from the other Cinque Ports were also summoned.

It was this, the first known assembly in which the ordinary people of England were called upon to represent their boroughs, that has made this parliament of 20 January, 1265, a landmark in our history; and it has made the name of Simon de Montfort live for ever in the annals of our constitution.

The proceedings of this famous parliament began late and continued slowly. The knights of Shropshire and Staffordshire had not appeared even by the end of February. The knights who had arrived punctually began to feel the financial strain of their long sojourn, so that the council ordered the sheriffs to allow them reasonable expenses after consulting with their fellow knights in the shires.

Finally a form of peace was agreed on 8 March. The form of provisional government arranged after the battle of Lewes was to continue. The barons and vassals who had defied the king on the eve of that battle were to be received back again as his men. Prince Edward was to be released from captivity, but not from restraint; he must swear to maintain the form of government and to refrain from all attacks upon those who had brought it into being; he must bring no foreigners into the country and must join in repelling any who did come. He must not leave England for three years from the coming Easter. If he disobeyed these edicts he could be disinherited. His household, officers and castles were to be purged of suspects. He was to give over as hostages the great castles of Bristol, Dover, Scarborough, Bamborough, Nottingham and Corfe as guarantees of peace and his good faith.

The prince issued formal letters to record his sworn acceptance of the terms, and of the right of the barons to

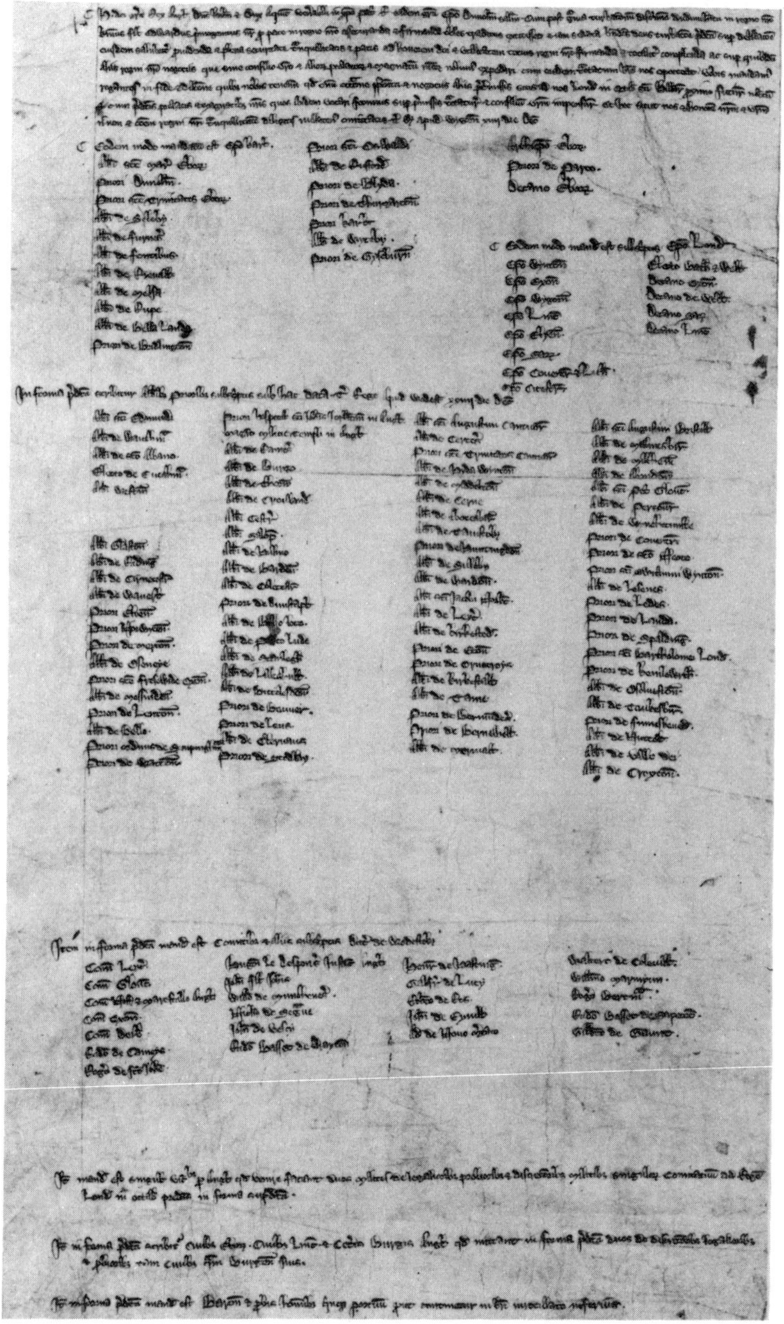

At the top is a copy of the writ sent to the bishop of Durham, dated 14 *December* 1264. *It tells how the king wishes to confer with the prelates and magnates concerning the liberation of his son and the restoration of peace, and "on certain other affairs of our kingdom which we do not wish to decide without your counsel and the counsel of our other prelates and magnates".*

The bishop is therefore required to be present in London on 20 *January* 1265. *There follows a list in four columns of the other bishops, abbots, priors and deans to whom the writ was also sent.*

After this comes a further list of abbots and the names of five earls and eighteen barons to whom writs were also sent. The names of the earls and barons are:

The Earl of Leicester
The Earl of Gloucester
The Earl of Norfolk (Marshal)
The Earl of Oxford
The Earl of Derby

Ralph de Camoys
Roger de St John
Hugh le Despenser (Justiciar)
John Fitz John
William de Munchanesy
Nicholas de Segrave
John de Vescy
Ralph Bassett of Drayton
Henry of Hastings
Geoffrey de Lucy
Robert de Ros
John D'Eyville
Adam of Newmarket
Walter de Colville
William Marmion
Roger Bertram
Ralph Bassett of Sapcote
Gilbert of Gaunt

Near the foot of the roll is the command to each sheriff of the thirty-seven shires of England to summon two knights to the parliament.

After this comes the crucial entry: "Letters are written in the preceding form to the citizens of York, the citizens of Lincoln and to other boroughs of England that they should send in the preceding manner two of the more discreet, lawful and trustworthy of their citizens or burgesses." And finally a similar entry for the "barons and trustworthy men of the Cinque Ports" is made.

resist him if he broke his word. The king issued letters to the same effect and both undertook to seek no way of absolution from their oaths. Both also bound themselves to the observance of Magna Carta.

The council was to proceed to deal with all the judicial business that had piled up during the recent disorders and steps were to be taken to re-open the wool trade with Flanders. Proclamations were issued to the leading exiles in their manors to return to answer for their conduct in a new parliament to be held on 1 June of that year.

Surely this was Simon de Montfort's finest hour! He must have seemed irresistible on that great day of 11 March, 1265 when, in Westminster Hall, the release of Prince Edward was announced and the solemn declarations of the king and his son were read to the waiting crowd. Every free man, it was declared, was now to renew his homage and fealty to the king, who had agreed to all the terms. Surely everything that Simon had striven and fought for was now accomplished and his work done!

Yet behind the impressive close of this famous parliament lurked an atmosphere of distrust and suspicion, and at no time was the great earl's position more precarious. Much that he did made him an object of hatred and suspicion. His enemies accused him of being a traitor not only to the king but to his peers "for puffing up the lowly people". Even some of the barons of his own party complained that he sought to have a king who reigned but did not govern and a chief minister, himself, who governed, but did not reign. But in order to clear the way for order and justice Simon was obliged to erect safeguards that smacked of tyranny. He could neither legalize his power nor could he surrender it without betraying all that he stood for. But the time was rapidly approaching when he could no longer rely on the loyalty of some of his supporters.

While the parliament was being held the earl of Gloucester had arranged a tournament to be held at

Dunstable in the middle of February, in which he and his retinue were to have met and competed with Earl Simon's sons. Hearing of this Earl Simon at once sternly forbade it. There was much enmity between the two and such tournaments could be dangerous. Only too easily could mock warfare among an armed assembly turn into the real thing. The young earl "Red" Gilbert of Gloucester, greedy and restless, flared into a violent rage at this order, claiming that all the money he had spent in preparing for the tournament would be wasted. He also accused Simon of granting all the royal castles to his own sons. It was true that Simon was too indulgent and fond a father, but he was forced to place the most important castles in the care of those he could trust and whatever their failings he could be sure of his sons' loyalty and devotion. It might have been better if Simon had soothed this violent young earl, his chief ally and support, with soft words and honeyed promises, but in his stern and uncompromising way and in a voice heavy with wrath he said that any who defied his orders, whoever they might be, he would have cast into a place where they could enjoy neither sun nor moon.

So hot did this quarrel grow that it caused the final fatal split in the barons' party. Withdrawing from parliament without leave and heading for his lands in the west, Gilbert de Clare, earl of Gloucester, and all his great following with him, changed sides.

XXIII

The End Approaches

THE DEFECTION of the earl of Gloucester was serious indeed and the danger to Simon grew. Yet we are told, "It was notorious that no one ever saw the earl in despair, or even downcast; he was like a mountain, strong, constant, immovable; wherefore he was rightly called de Montfort." But in spite of his steadfast determination his coming fate was inevitable and the end was not to be long delayed.

By the middle of March the parliament had broken up and Simon travelled to what was to be the last great gathering of his family at their castle of Odiham. He had the king and Prince Edward with him, still under restraint. They evidently travelled in some state for they had 300 horses with them on this occasion. On 2 April he left Odiham and, taking with him the king and Prince Edward, headed for the west. He was never to see his wife the countess again. She was doing what she could to rally support for him in the east and finally settled herself in Dover castle.

Simon left Prince Edward in custody at Hereford and now he heard that the earl of Gloucester had taken the final step in opposing him. He had joined forces with Roger Mortimer, Lord of the Marchers, in the west. He was an old and bitter enemy of Simon's and together he and the earl of Gloucester planned to fight Simon and free the king.

Their first move was to try and rescue Prince Edward. The prince had been given permission by Simon to go outside the city walls for daily exercise. His friends had sent him a magnificent horse as a present, and on a day secretly arranged he suggested to his guards that they should ride races while he acted as umpire. He waited until their horses were all utterly blown and winded, while his of course remained perfectly fresh; then, bidding them a contemptuous farewell, he galloped off at great speed and did not draw rein until he had reached the safety of the Mortimer castle, some twenty miles away.

The earl of Gloucester met the prince at Ludlow and swore allegiance to him, after having first induced him to vow once more that he would observe the ancient laws of the land and would never introduce foreigners to power.

Prince Edward now became the centre to which all the royalist elements in the land flocked – the old royalists, the unruly Marchers, and the moderates under the earl of Gloucester – and the future looked black indeed for Simon de Montfort. His danger was acute, though all would not have been lost had it not been for the folly of his younger son Simon. His father had sent him to raise troops in the south and east, especially in London, and then to march to his aid. This he did, early in July, but instead of then marching straight to the west he turned southwards again and wasted precious time in an attempt on Winchester with the object of collecting funds and men. Loyal to the king, the citizens of that city refused to let him in, whereupon he sacked and pillaged it. Then he pursued his journey by way of Oxford and Northampton, both of which towns showed themselves friendly, or at least neutral. Marching thus by easy stages he arrived at Kenilworth in the last days of July.

Meanwhile great crowds of supporters had joined Prince Edward as he marched on Worcester, Bridgnorth and Shrewsbury, and down the Severn valley, burning bridges, carrying off boats and blocking fords, determined to hem in Simon's forces behind the line of the river Severn. Gloucester, the last crossing over the Severn, fell to Prince Edward after a gallant resistance by the garrison there.

Despairing of all other help, Earl Simon then made an alliance with Prince Llywelyn of Wales, who promised him 5,000 Welsh spearmen in return for border lands. Trapped behind the river Severn and defeated by Prince Edward's forces wherever they tried to cross it, Simon's men still had one last way out. Bristol castle was in the prince's hands, but the townspeople were friendly to Simon. They offered to supply him with ships to get his army across the Bristol channel and thus to open up the road to London. The ships were to be sent to Newport, but Prince Edward, sallying forth from Gloucester, fell upon them in great strength and destroyed them. So vanished in smoke and flame Simon's last chance to get across the Bristol channel and on to London.

Under cover of night Earl Simon left Newport and retreated northwards again. His men suffered terribly from hunger, since thin milk and stringy mutton was all that the desolate Welsh country could provide and they were wearied out by the difficult marches through wooded and trackless country. They entered Hereford again and there gathered fresh horses and supplies; but Simon knew that he must get across the barrier of the Severn river and try to reach Kenilworth or London to meet the desperately needed reinforcements that his son, Simon the younger, was bringing to meet him.

Meanwhile, Simon the younger, having reached Kenilworth late in the evening and finding his army too numerous to get inside the castle, had scattered his troops about the village and in the priory. He and most of his barons also lay outside the castle, finding there more comfortable quarters.

Prince Edward, lying at Worcester, heard from his scouts, one of whom was a woman called Margot dressed in men's clothing, of the arrival of Simon the younger with his army at Kenilworth. He decided to make a hazardous night march and to launch a surprise attack upon him and his army of reinforcements.

Withdrawing all his forces from the river line he made a rapid night march and arrived outside Kenilworth by dawn.

They marched into the village and Simon the younger's forces were so taken by surprise that they made little or no resistance. They were roused from their beds by cries: "Get up! Get up, ye traitors! Come out, or by the death of God ye are all undone!" A few made their escape by back ways and fled, some stark naked, some with only their breeches on, others carrying their clothes under their arms, while many were seized in their beds. Almost naked, young Simon himself escaped with difficulty by boat across the lake and so got safely into

the castle. Huge numbers of prisoners were taken, including many nobles, and the booty was immense. So many horses were captured that Prince Edward was able to turn his infantry into cavalry and the very grooms paraded themselves before him with the armour and on the war-horses of knights.

This blow was to be fatal to Simon de Montfort and decided the outcome of the war; for though Kenilworth itself could not be taken the larger half of the barons' army was destroyed and Prince Edward was now free to fall upon the remainder with overpowering force.

XXIV

The Last Battle

EARL Simon, weary of waiting for the aid that never came and unconscious of his son's defeat, was surprised to find that Prince Edward and his forces had left Worcester. He at once seized the chance of ferrying his army unopposed across the Severn river near Kempsy, four miles south of Worcester. From there he intended marching to Kenilworth to join his son, if he did not meet him on the road.

On 3 August the earl and his army finished the day's march at the little town of Evesham, which was almost enclosed by a loop of the river Avon. Here they rested for the night at the abbey. The aged captive king, who had become a mere puppet and figurehead, was tired and the whole army needed food. The monks in the abbey served the best of their food and wine to them and the knights and men-at-arms eased themselves out of the weight of their helmets and mail armour, and washed off the hot August dust in the cool river.

At dawn next day all crowded to the abbey to hear mass and to be blessed by the bishop of Worcester. The summer's day had dawned hot but dark and sultry, and heavy clouds hung oppressively over the little town. Earl Simon gave the order to mount and prepare to march on to Kenilworth. Did any shadow of foreboding warn him that for him and his followers there was to be

This stained-glass window in St Lawrence's church, Evesham, depicts Simon de Montfort and his knights receiving communion before the battle.

no road out of Evesham? A few large and heavy drops of rain fell through the still air from the overcast sky and splashed onto the mail armour of the knights and men-at-arms as they made ready to move off. The very air was dark with menace and the scene was set for tragedy. Uneasily Earl Simon sent his barber Nicholas, a man noted for his keen eyesight and who knew every banner and blazon in England, up to the tower of the abbey to see if he could see in the distance the longed-for army of his son.

Suddenly the barber shouted down that he could see troops of horsemen approaching from several directions through the folds of the hills. Seconds later he cried that he could see the banners of Simon the younger and his partisans floating in the van of the advancing force.

A sigh of relief floated through the serried ranks as Earl Simon exclaimed with joy, "It is my son!"

But another minute and Nicholas the barber saw with horror the leopard banners of Prince Edward and the blue and white blazons of Mortimer. Their enemies were upon them and in overwhelming numbers. They carried the thirteen banners of the young Simon's army, captured at Kenilworth, only to deceive them.

Despairingly Nicholas the barber shouted down to Earl Simon "We are all dead men, for it is not your son who comes as you thought, but the king's son from one part, the earl of Gloucester from another, and Roger Mortimer from the third."

At last the final fatal encounter had come. Simon and his army were caught in a trap. Hemmed in on all sides by the foe and the river encircling the little town, Earl Simon faced his army and said, "Let us commend our souls to God, for our bodies are theirs."

Outnumbered as they were by seven to two all realized that there could be no hope of victory and that this was the end.

More bitter than the thought of his own fate must have

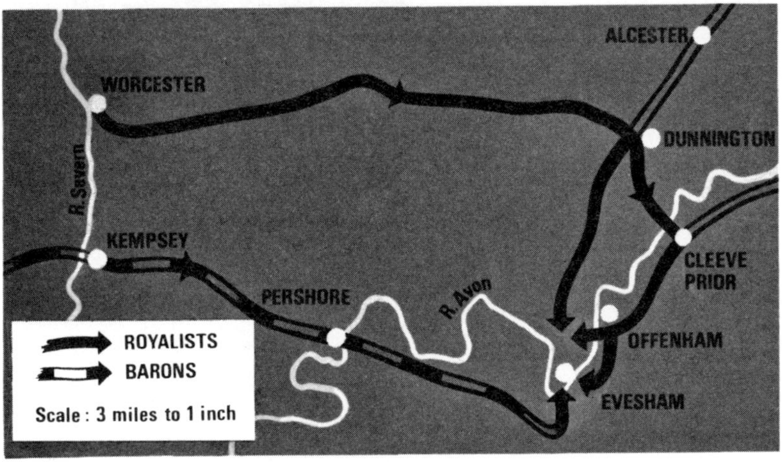

The approach marches to Evesham, 1–4 *August* 1265.

been to Simon the conviction that the cause for which he had risked so much was doomed to perish with him. Did any moment of vision flash across his mind that in years to come others as great and more fortunate than he would arise to protect the liberties of the country he had adopted for his own?

But this was no time for dreams; he would sell his life as dearly as he could. His friends urged him to fly, but the thought of safety for himself was not in his mind. He tried to persuade his son Henry, who offered to bear the brunt of the battle in his stead, and the other leaders to escape while there was yet time; but love and honour are ever deaf to such arguments and all remained to perish.

"Come then," said the earl, "and let us die like men; for we have fasted here and we shall breakfast in heaven." Then he led his army out against the enemy with the white crosses again upon their shoulders and in as close order as he could. In their midst rode the king, armed, and with a helmet on his head.

As they rode forth from the little town towards the hills outside they came into full view of the massed strength of Prince Edward's army, ranged all around them on the rising ridges.

"By the arm of St James!" Earl Simon exclaimed, "They come on well! That they learned not of themselves, they learned from me."

Prince Edward had indeed deployed his army well, with the earl of Gloucester joining him from the north-western side and Mortimer coming up behind. In every direction and in great depth the barons' small army was encircled.

Earl Simon raised his sword, trumpets blared forth the charge, and at full gallop the little army hurled itself upon the enemy. Headed by the mailed knights on heavy chargers, they crashed into the centre of the royalist line, where Prince Edward and the earl of Gloucester's divisions joined. This first savage onslaught forced the

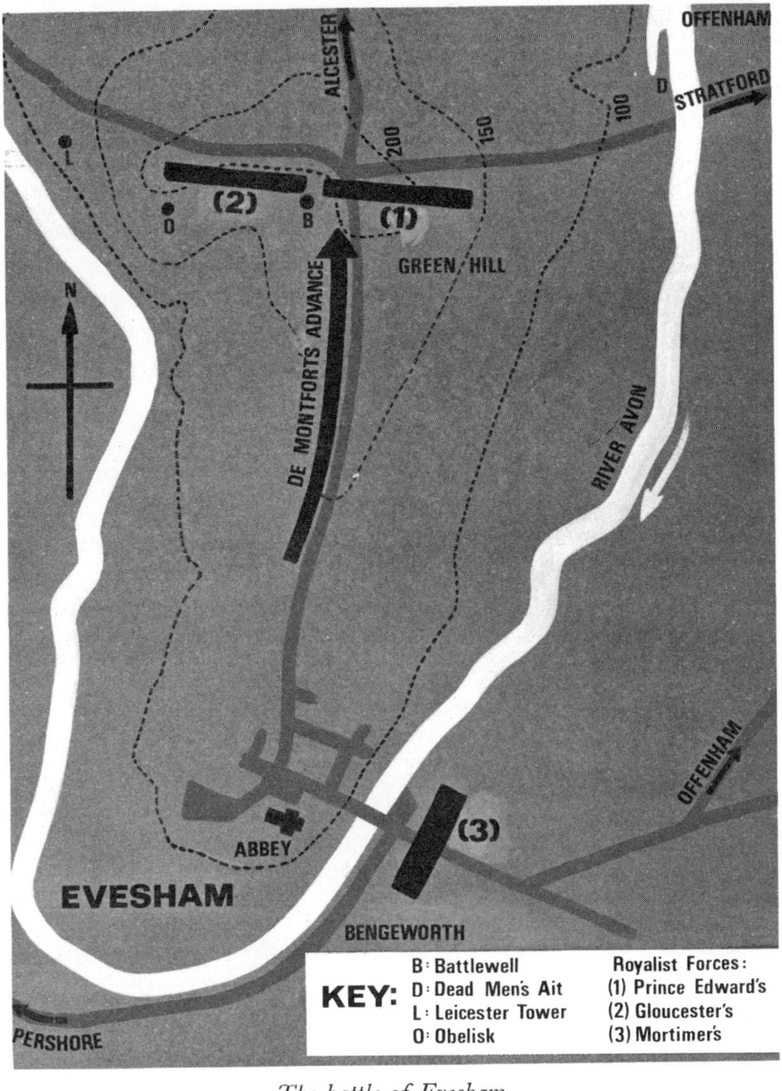

The battle of Evesham.

royalists to give ground, but their cavalry upon the extreme wings charged upon the Welsh foot soldiers supporting Simon in the rear. These broke ranks and fled to the river Avon, where many drowned. The unequal battle raged for several hours. The shrill screaming of the wounded horses rose above the savage battle cries as knights and men-at-arms hacked and battled at close quarters. King Henry, wounded in the shoulder in the thick of the battle, only saved himself by raising his helmet and shouting repeatedly, "I am Henry of Winchester, your king! Do not harm me!" The royalists heard and dragged him safely from the battle.

Earl Simon, despite his fifty-eight years, fought with great bravery, charging through the enemy ranks on his great war-horse, his knights beside him, hewing and hacking their way forward. Soon his horse was killed under him and word was brought to him that Gloucester's soldiers had killed his son Henry.

"Is it so?" he cried, "then indeed it is time for me to die."

Wielding his huge two-edged sword with both hands he laid about him with so terrific a force that had there been but half a dozen more like himself, said one who saw the fight, he would have turned the tide of battle. But it was not to be.

Everywhere Prince Edward's knights, with red crosses on their white surcoats, began to surround the Blanche Lion standard where the great earl stood like a tower and to close in round him for the kill. His dearest friends were all around him as if to defend him with the rampart of their bodies, but one by one they dropped in death.

"Traitor! Surrender!" his foes roared.

"Never will I surrender to dogs and perjurers, but to God alone," Simon's answer rang out. Sword in hand and fighting to the last, he finally fell when a foot soldier, lifting up his coat of mail from behind, stabbed him in the back, and with the words "Dieu merci" on his lips, he died.

The battle then became a butchery. No quarter was asked or given. In a frenzy of hatred and blood-lust the vindictive slaughter continued until at length the few survivors of the barons' army scattered.

Prince Edward's soldiers searched the field, stripping

The mutilation of Simon de Montfort's body at the battle of Evesham.

and robbing the dead. They found among them some baronial leaders still alive and saved them in the hope of ransoms. In this way Guy de Montfort, third son of Earl Simon, fell into royalist hands and became a prisoner. Orders were given to the royalist soldiers to bury the dead and the monks from Evesham buried many in and around the abbey. Prince Edward wept at the burial of Henry de Montfort, his cousin and boyhood friend, but he would have no mercy shown to the corpse of Earl Simon. His body was cut up piecemeal, mangled and mutilated. The head was stuck upon a lance point and carried by a rider, together with the hands, as a bloody sign of victory, to Roger Mortimer's wife at Wigmore. "May St John the Baptist, precursor of the Lord, whose head was served up at a banquet to please the dancer Salome, help the sender's soul," comments the chronicler William Rishanger.

Simon the younger, hastening too late from Kenilworth with what reinforcements he had been able to muster, met this grisly trophy of victory upon the road. He returned in anguish to Kenilworth, there to mourn bitterly and for many days would neither eat nor drink.

When the bearer of this fearful trophy reached Wigmore he found that the Lady Mortimer was not in the castle. She was at mass in the neighbouring abbey and thither the messenger followed her, still carrying the head and with the maimed hands sewn up in a cloth thrust into his bosom. He rushed into the abbey in the eagerness of his zeal and whispered the tidings of the victory into the ears of the devout lady. At the moment of the raising up of the Host, the hands of Simon de Montfort were seen by the whole congregation to be raised up over the messenger's head clasped together in prayer, though they were afterwards found within the cloth bag as before, with its stitches undisturbed.

The mangled remains of Earl Simon's body were gathered together by sorrowing monks, wrapped in a cloth and carried on a hurdle to the abbey to be buried at the foot of the high altar there.

"Such was the murder of Evesham, for battle it was none." Thus did the shocked chroniclers of the times describe that desperate day. One of them, Robert of Gloucester, who was there, describes how the day was hot and heavy, dark and overcast, with large unnatural drops of rain. Later violent thunder storms and great bolts of lightning raged throughout the day and the accompanying darkness was so thick that the monks could no longer see to chant their prayers. He ends: "This saw Robert . . . and was very sore afraid."

XXV

The End of the Struggle

When the news of the great earl's death spread over England there was great lamentation and sorrow among the people that their champion and the defender of their freedom was no more. In royalist eyes he might be a traitorous felon, but in many a house of friars and nuns and among the common people he became a martyr and a saint. For them and for countless others he had been the protector of the poor and the upholder of justice. His legend grew, his tomb became a place of pilgrimage and songs were made about him which lingered in the memories of local singers for many years. Stories of miracles, numbering 212, which took place near or around the place of his death, began to spread. In a hollow of the hill where the battle of Evesham took place there was a small spring which was afterwards called the Earl's well, or Battle well, or de Montfort's well. According to local tradition it ran with blood instead of water after the battle. Later on many cures were said to have taken place in animals as well as men when they drank of the water of that spring.

Within a few months of his death stories that his foot, encased in silver and preserved at Alnwick abbey, had cured a wealthy burgess of Newcastle on Tyne of almost total paralysis and of similar miracles became widespread.

For the character of Simon de Montfort we cannot do

Battle well as it is today – overgrown and neglected.

better than read the words of William Rishanger, monk of St Albans, and one of the most active historical chroniclers with first-hand knowledge of him.

He was indeed a mighty man, and prudent and circumspect; in the use of arms and in experience of warfare superior to all others of his time; commendably endowed with knowledge of letters; fond of hearing the offices of the church by day and night; sparing of food and drink, as those about him saw with their own eyes; in time of night watching more than he slept, as his more intimate friends have oft related.

In the greatest difficulties which he went through while handling affairs of state he was found trustworthy, notably in Gascony, whither he went by command of the king, and there subdued to the king's majesty rebels before time unconquered, and sent them to England to his lord the king.

He was moreover pleasant and witty in speech, and ever aimed at the reward of an admirable faith; on account of which he did not fear to undergo death, as shall be told hereafter.

His constancy all men, even his enemies, admired; for when others had sworn to observe the Provisions of Oxford, and the most part of them despised and rejected that to which they had sworn he having once taken the oath, like an immovable pillar, stood firm, and neither by threats, nor promises, nor gifts, nor flattery could be moved to depart in any way with the other magnates from the oath which he had taken to reform the state of the realm.

He commended himself to the prayers of the religious, and humbly as with brotherly affection, he begged to be allied with them, in the pouring out of prayers to God for the State of the realm and the peace of the church; and he was constant in supplication that divine grace might keep him spotless from avarice and covetousness of earthly things, knowing for a surety that many in those days were encumbered by such vices, as the issue of things afterwards made clear.

To the religious and other prelates of the church, commended by honesty of life, he showed all due reverence; deserving to be called the perfect disciple of a perfect Master; having been instructed in all good discipline, inasmuch as he clung with hearty affection to the blessed Robert, once bishop of Lincoln, and gave his children to be brought up by him, and did many things by his wholesome advice. And the said bishop is related to have enjoined upon the earl, for the remission of his sins that he should take upon himself that cause for which he fought even unto death; declaring that the peace of the English church could never be secured without the temporal sword, and constantly affirming all who died in her and for her should receive the crown of martyrdom.

It is related by trustworthy persons, that the bishop once placed his hands on the head of the earl's firstborn son and said to him, "My dearest son, thou and thy father shall both die on one day and by one hurt, for the cause of justice." And of what sort was the life of the bishop, the miracles done by the grace of God at his tomb sufficiently declare. And the earl, like a second Joshua, worshipped justice, as the very medicine of his soul.

The barons' war was not quite finished by the battle of Evesham. The followers of Simon de Montfort,

Dover castle.

scattered though they were, continued the hopeless struggle against the royal forces for more than two years, and they became known as the Disinherited.

Immediately after the victory of Evesham King Henry again took the government into his own hands and lost no time in following up his success. Within a few weeks after the death of Earl Simon, not satisfied by the terrible revenge taken upon the field of Evesham, King Henry summoned a council at Winchester at which punishment was meted out to the survivors with an unsparing hand. The whole family of de Montfort and of all his partisans were outlawed and their property confiscated.

Earl Simon's wife, the countess of Leicester, received the tragic news of the death of her husband and eldest son while she was at Dover castle. Putting on a russet robe of mourning she sent in her grief messages to her brother the king pleading for mercy for herself and her remaining children. But the king would have nothing to do with his sister and never spoke her name again. So she sailed with her children out of Dover harbour to France, where she took refuge in the Dominican convent of Montargis and was never to see England again.

Simon the younger, now the eldest surviving son of the great earl, did not allow his grief and remorse at the loss his own folly had caused to overpower him for long. In the months before the battle of Evesham his father had stocked Kenilworth with all the best equipment to withstand a siege, as well as arms, suits of chain mail, horses, and great stores of food and wine. Simon the younger now added to these with all that he could muster in the country around Kenilworth and he awaited the siege that he knew would come.

The defenders of Kenilworth held out with grim determination for many months against the large army that Prince Edward sent to blockade them. There were well over a thousand men within the castle and fifty-three of their wives and handmaidens. Some of the incidents of this long siege, a mixture of savage vengeance and chivalrous courtesy, are characteristic of war in those days. On one occasion the besieged within the castle walls cut off the hand of the royal herald who had come from the king to tell them to surrender and they sent the hand to the king as a present from the Disinherited. At another time when a wounded royalist prisoner died inside the castle his enemies carried him forth in honourable procession with lighted tapers, and placed the corpse outside the castle walls so that his friends might bury him in peace.

Great trenches were cut round the castle to hem in the defenders and huge wooden towers holding slingers and bowmen, one especially called a Bear from its size, were advanced forward; barges were transported overland from Chester to assist in the assault across the castle lake, but the defenders successfully resisted these efforts with mangonels and other engines.

The stores however dwindled day by day and sickness and starvation took its toll. Finally there came a day when even the last horse had been devoured and hunger compelled the gallant survivors to surrender. Prince Edward, in admiration for their bravery, persuaded his father to grant them generous terms, and by the Kenilworth Dictum (or decree) they were able to obtain pardon by the payment of fines.

With the surrender of Kenilworth in December 1267 the barons' war came to an end. Simon the younger and his brother Guy de Montfort, who had recovered from his battle wounds and escaped from his royalist

gaolers by bribing them, left England as exiles and went to Italy, to remake their fortunes. This they did with the help of a cousin from another branch of the powerful de Montfort family. Guy distinguished himself at the battle of Alba and won the admiration of Charles of Anjou, who made him his viceroy of Florence and Tuscany. He married the daughter of the "Red" Count Aldebrandini, so called from the fiery colour of his hair, and thus became allied with one of the chief families of the province. Both brothers however were soon to shock all Europe by a murderous act of barbarity. Their cousin Henry of Almain arrived in Vitero on various errands for his father, Richard of Cornwall, and King Henry. The two de Montforts could not forget that Henry of Almain had deserted their father before the battle of Lewes and the sight of him roused their passions to fury. Henry had risen early and gone to the church of San Lorenzo to hear mass. Afterwards he continued kneeling alone in prayer before the high altar. Suddenly the sound of mailed feet in the nave aroused him and loud angry voices shouted "Traitor! Murderer of our father! Remember Evesham!"

Still on his knees Henry reeled under the heavy blows of their broadswords as Guy and Simon de Montfort and the Count Aldebrandini slashed furiously at him. One blow split his skull while another struck the hand with which he was clinging to the altar as he tried to rise and left three of the fingers on it. Then the three murderers dragged Henry by his hair out into the bright sunshine to die and made good their escape.

Neither brother however outlived the disgrace of this bloody deed. Simon died soon afterwards in hiding and Guy ended his days in the darkness of an Italian dungeon.

The great Simon de Montfort's only daughter later married Prince Llywelyn of Wales, but died in childbirth, her little daughter being brought up by nuns. She never married and with her death perished the last direct descendant of the great earl.

XXVI

Victory in Defeat

HAD William the Conqueror been able to foresee the future and had this shown him the blustery January day in 1265 when Simon de Montfort's parliament met in Westminster Hall, he would hardly have recognized his Great Council in this motley collection of barons and prelates, knights and burgesses, who came from far and wide in answer to their leader's summons. A stern and autocratic ruler himself, he might have had little sympathy for the captive King Henry. Possibly he would have admired Simon's resolute qualities, and would have urged him to depose Henry and make himself king by force of arms, just as he, William, had done two centuries before. Most probably he would have been aghast at the aggressive self-confidence and independence of thought obvious among many members of this parliament. His policy had been to keep his barons in subjection to himself; they had been dependent on him for their lands and positions. However, Henry III's barons were demanding control over the king, and the right to choose his counsellors.

William's Great Councils had given him opportunities to explain his policies to the whole assembly, and thus ensure their co-operation: he had not asked for criticism or even free discussion. The members of Edward I's parliaments, 200 years later, had a far more positive rôle to play. The greater and better men among them considered that they were there not only to protect their own interests, but to make sure that the kingdom was ruled in the interests of all its inhabitants. Of course most of them were too selfish to take any notice of interests that were not their own, and many members, especially the knights and burgesses, took little or no part in the discussions. The important thing is that this collection of landowners, townsmen and churchmen was slowly beginning to feel that it had a certain influence on the king, and a positive rôle to play in the government of England.

There is so much talk today of "one man, one vote" that we tend to forget that people have not always felt that they have the right either to help choose the government of their country, or even to be directly represented in that government. In the middle ages such an idea would have been very strange. Most people had no wish to take part in the government of England: so long as they were left in peace and safety, with their commerce, industry and agriculture protected and their freedom of action untouched, then they wished for little more. They were involved in their own affairs, perhaps even in shire or borough administration, and Westminster was a distant thought and an uncomfortable journey away, a far cry from the humdrum business of everyday life.

Though the barons had been defeated by the royalist triumph at Evesham, the cause for which they and Simon de Montfort had fought was not lost; rather, in the fullness of time, it triumphed. For Prince Edward, well understanding the English and being one of those whom revolutions teach, learnt from this struggle that the only way to rule a strong and united people was to take frequent counsel with their chosen representatives. Edward realized that much of the trouble since 1200 had been caused by lack of trust between the king and his barons. The barons had been excluded from the task of government and had not had faith that this government would be in the interests either of them or of the country.

Naturally most of them cared more for themselves than for the country. In their turn, King John and King Henry III had mistrusted the barons and had feared that they might join in league against their rulers – as indeed they tried to do. Edward I sought to rule *with* his subjects in the interests of a larger part of the community. With this in mind he continued Simon de Montfort's tradition of summoning more representative parliaments. He saw that the best way to prevent quarrels and misunderstandings was to discuss policies with his magnates, so that they should feel involved and should be able to voice their own opinions.

King Edward quickly saw the advantages of a more widely representative collection of members in his parliaments. The borough and county members could help him in assessing and collecting taxes, for he was always short of money. In parliament he could explain to them how these taxes were for the benefit of the whole country. The members would then return home and explain the king's policy to their neighbours, who had no other means of information. They would also inform the king of local grievances and of the needs of each community, and of the misdeeds of bad government officials. This helped Edward to bring just and honest government to every Englishman.

In these ways the king hoped to ensure the loyal cooperation of his subjects. From Earl Simon he learnt to value the support of the middle classes, with their growing wealth and influence in countryside and town.

In 1267 the Statute of Marlborough was passed, and this embodied many of the reforms that the barons had promised to put into practice in their Provisions of Oxford. These were aimed largely at giving the smaller landowners security of tenure and protecting them from the greed of unscrupulous royal officials. He knew that if the community felt secure in possession of its rights and belongings, then England would prosper. Of course the Statute did not include those reforms which had

The parliament of Edward I.

attempted to limit the king's power, for Edward believed in strong kingship.

He succeeded where his uncle had not because he was the rightful king of England, and Simon could claim no real right to govern – only the ability. Many magnates had regarded Simon as an upstart. His over-bearing manner and arrogance had aroused jealousy and hatred. But Edward was their lawful king, and these barons were royalist at heart. They had always protested that they did not fight the king, but only his evil advisers. Edward, as their king, could unite them all behind him, and with their support could achieve the reforms for which his uncle had worked.

Thus the end of Simon de Montfort's story does not come with his death. Now, 700 years later, our parliament has grown from those beginnings into what it is today, the model for most of the world's free constitutions; and Simon de Montfort, dying for his ideals on the field of Evesham, did not die in vain.

Acknowledgements

The authors and publisher would like to thank the following for permitting the reproduction of copyright photographs:
B. T. Batsford Ltd, page 150; British Travel Association, page 19; Central Office of Information, Crown Copyright, page 140; D. C. Cox, B.A., page 148; French Government Tourist Office, pages 17 and 64; Mansell Collection, page 109; National Monuments Record, Crown Copyright, page 84; Radio Times Hulton Picture Library, pages 55 and 157; Guy Rivière, page 66; Trustees of the British Museum, pages v, 12, 24/25, 75 and 145; Warburg Institute, photo Helmut Gernsheim, page 28. The facsimiles on pages 49 and 130 of Crown-copyright records in the Public Record Office appear by permission of the Controller of H.M. Stationery Office.

Index